$\mathscr{T}$o

_____

$\mathscr{F}$ROM

_____

$\mathscr{M}$ESSAGE

_____

_____

_____

_____

Promises from God for When You Hurt

© 2003 Christian Art Gifts, RSA
Christian Art Gifts, Lombard, IL

Compiled by Wilma Le Roux and Lynette Douglas
Designed by Christian Art Gifts

ISBN 1-86920-071-3

Printed in China

03 04 05 06 07 08 09 10 11 12 – 10 9 8 7 6 5 4 3 2 1

PROMISES
FROM GOD FOR
WHEN YOU
HURT

christian
art gifts

Contents

INTRODUCTION

Cast your cares on the LORD and he will sustain you; he will never let the righteous fall.

Psalm 55:22, NIV

It's a wonderful truth that God is always ready, willing, and able to bear the burden of the hurts and disappointments that life brings our way. The Bible doesn't say that our cares need to be momentous or life-shattering – God promises to bear the tiny and the big burdens that we have. We can bring any and every detail of our lives to God – whether it be physical, emotional or spiritual, God's Word has a promise that can bring comfort and encouragement to your hurting heart.

As we meditate on the promises of God, we will draw near to Him and find peace in the midst of turmoil, hope in the midst of chaos. Whatever you are facing, whether grief, injustice, or loneliness, the Bible assures us that God knows and cares, and He holds your future in His hands.

ABANDONMENT

God has said, "Never will I leave you; never will I forsake you."

Hebrews 13:5, NIV

Loneliness has been a problem since the beginning of time. And people try to flee from the pain of loneliness through many ways.

However hard we try to anesthetize the pain, it always reemerges, often in the sleepless hours of the early morning, when we face problems, or when we are run down.

You can actively drive loneliness from your life by being positive about yourself, your abilities, and your acceptability. Enjoy your own company. Do things for yourself: buy yourself flowers or little gifts. Always look your best – groom yourself and dress tastefully. Plan things to do that will enrich your spirit. Cultivate meaningful relationships with other people. Be friendly. Be interested in others.

Above all, develop a deep awareness of the presence of Jesus Christ. If He is your constant companion you will never be lonely.

GOD'S PROMISES

FOR THE ABANDONED

Do not hide Your face from me; do not turn Your servant away in anger; You have been my help; do not leave me nor forsake me, O God of my salvation. When my father and my mother forsake me, then the Lord will take care of me.

Psalm 27:9-10, NKJV

Do not cast me off in the time of old age; forsake me not when my strength is spent. For my enemies speak concerning me; those who watch for my life consult together and say, "God has forsaken him; pursue and seize him, for there is none to deliver him." O God, be not far from me; O my God, make haste to help me! With the mighty deeds of the LORD GOD I will come; I will remind them of your righteousness, yours alone. And my tongue will talk of your righteous help all the day long, for they have been put to shame and disappointed who sought to do me hurt.

Psalm 71:9-12, 16, 24, ESV

And they that know thy name will put their trust in thee: for thou, LORD, hast not forsaken them that seek thee.

Psalm 9:10, KJV

"Can a mother forget the baby at her breast and have no compassion on the child she has borne? Though she may forget, I will not forget you! See, I have engraved you on the palms of my hands; your walls are ever before me."

Isaiah 49:15-16, NIV

When the poor and needy seek water, and there is none, and their tongue faileth for thirst, I the LORD will hear them, I the God of Israel will not forsake them. I will open rivers in high places, and fountains in the midst of the valleys: I will make the wilderness a pool of water, and the dry land springs of water.

Isaiah 41:17-18, KJV

I have been young, and now am old; yet have I not seen the righteous forsaken, nor his seed begging bread.

Psalm 37:25, KJV

"For you are a holy people to the LORD your God; the LORD your God has chosen you to be a people for Himself, a special treasure above all the peoples on the face of the earth. Therefore know that the LORD your God, He is God, the faithful God who keeps covenant and mercy for a thousand generations with those who love Him and keep His commandments."

Deuteronomy 7:6, 9, NKJV

Be strong and of a good courage, fear not, nor be afraid of them: for the LORD thy God, he it is that doth go with thee; he will not fail thee, nor forsake thee.

Deuteronomy 31:6, KJV

"I am with you always, even to the end of the age."

Matthew 28:20, NKJV

For the LORD your God is a merciful God; he will not abandon or destroy you or forget the covenant with your forefathers, which he confirmed to them by oath.

Deuteronomy 4:31, NIV

$\mathscr{A}$BUSE

You are my hiding place; you will protect me from trouble and surround me with songs of deliverance.

Psalm 32:7, NIV

Often it seems that the more we live a godly and holy life, the more we are attacked for our moral standards, and face persecution for our faith in Christ. We should not be surprised, as the Bible reminds us, when this happens, as we belong to the Kingdom of God which is at enmity with the systems of the world.

God assures us that He is not unaware of the abuse we face for His sake. He hears every word spoken against us, and feels every ache of our heart as though His own heart were being broken.

And He offers us a place of safety in His arms, a hiding place where we can shelter from the storms of life. From the security of His presence we can know peace because He will avenge us, He will establish us, and He will keep us from the evil one.

Hope from the Word

for the abused

O my God, in you I trust; let me not be put to shame; let not my enemies exult over me. Indeed, none who wait for you shall be put to shame; they shall be ashamed who are wantonly treacherous. My eyes are ever toward the LORD, for he will pluck my feet out of the net. Oh, guard my soul, and deliver me! Let me not be put to shame, for I take refuge in you.

Psalm 25:2-3, 15, 20, ESV

O LORD my God, in thee do I put my trust: save me from all them that persecute me, and deliver me: Oh let the wickedness of the wicked come to an end; but establish the just: for the righteous God trieth the hearts and reins. My defence is of God, which saveth the upright in heart.

Psalm 7:1, 9-10, KJV

"I do not pray that You should take them out of the world, but that You should keep them from the evil one."

John 17:15, NKJV

It is God who avenges me, and subdues the peoples under me; He delivers me from my enemies. You also lift me up above those who rise against me; You have delivered me from the violent man.

Psalm 18:47-48, NKJV

He rescued me from my strong enemy and from those who hated me, for they were too mighty for me. They confronted me in the day of my calamity, but the LORD was my support. He brought me out into a broad place; he rescued me, because he delighted in me.

Psalm 18:17-19, ESV

The eternal God is your refuge, and underneath are the everlasting arms. He will drive out your enemy before you, saying, 'Destroy him!'

Deuteronomy 33:27, NIV

"Blessed are you when they revile and persecute you, and say all kinds of evil against you falsely for My sake. Rejoice and be exceedingly glad, for great is your reward in heaven, for so they persecuted the prophets who were before you."

Matthew 5:11-12, NKJV

O LORD, how many are my foes! How many rise up against me! Many are saying of me, "God will not deliver him." Selah But you are a shield around me, O LORD; you bestow glory on me and lift up my head.

Psalm 3:1-3, NIV

Be pleased, O LORD, to deliver me: O LORD, make haste to help me. Let them be ashamed and confounded together that seek after my soul to destroy it; let them be driven backward and put to shame that wish me evil. Let them be desolate for a reward of their shame that say unto me, Aha, aha.

Psalm 40:13-15, KJV

But the LORD is with me as a dread warrior; therefore my persecutors will stumble; they will not overcome me. They will be greatly shamed, for they will not succeed. Their eternal dishonor will never be forgotten.

Jeremiah 20:11, ESV

"But whoso shall offend one of these little ones which believe in me, it were better for him that a millstone were hanged about his neck, and that he were drowned in the depth of the sea."

Matthew 18:6, KJV

$\mathscr{A}$LCOHOL

Wine is a mocker, strong drink a brawler, and whoever is led astray by it is not wise.

Proverbs 20:1, ESV

As the stresses of modern living take their toll on our lives, substance abuse and addiction steadily rises. In spite of large scale media wars waged against the excessive use of alcohol, more and more people turn to these chemical stimulants to help them cope, or to help them escape their lives.

Although you won't find any verse in the Bible that definitely forbids drinking wine or other alcoholic beverages, the Bible is clear that those who let alcohol control them are less than wise. Rather than resorting to alcohol or drugs, Christians should be "filled with the Spirit", and so will find joy, peace and strength far superior to the false courage and temporary "high" of any drink or drug.

The Word's view

on alcohol

Jesus and his disciples had also been invited to the wedding. When the wine was gone, Jesus' mother said to him, "They have no more wine."

John 2:2-3, NIV

Bread is made for laughter, and wine gladdens life.

Ecclesiastes 10:19, ESV

Noah began to be a man of the soil, and he planted a vineyard. He drank of the wine and became drunk and lay uncovered in his tent.

Genesis 9:20-21, ESV

Woe unto them that rise up early in the morning, that they may follow strong drink; that continue until night, till wine inflame them! And the harp, and the viol, the tabret, and pipe, and wine, are in their feasts: but they regard not the work of the Lord, neither consider the operation of his hands.

Isaiah 5:11-12, KJV

So he went to him and bandaged his wounds, pouring on oil and wine.

Luke 10:34, NKJV

"It is not for kings, O Lemuel – not for kings to drink wine, not for rulers to crave beer, lest they drink and forget what the law decrees, and deprive all the oppressed of their rights."

Proverbs 31:4-5, NIV

Speak unto the children of Israel, and say unto them, When either man or woman shall separate themselves to vow a vow of a Nazarite, to separate themselves unto the Lord: He shall separate himself from wine and strong drink, and shall drink no vinegar of wine, or vinegar of strong drink, neither shall he drink any liquor of grapes, nor eat moist grapes, or dried.

Numbers 6:2-3, KJV

Let us walk properly, as in the day, not in revelry and drunkenness, not in lewdness and lust, not in strife and envy.

Romans 13:13, NKJV

Be not drunk with wine, wherein is excess; but be filled with the Spirit.

Ephesians 5:18, KJV

Who has woe? Who has sorrow? Who has strife? Who has complaining? Who has wounds without cause? Who has redness of eyes? Those who tarry long over wine; those who go to try mixed wine. Do not look at wine when it is red, when it sparkles in the cup and goes down smoothly. In the end it bites like a serpent and stings like an adder. Your eyes will see strange things, and your heart utter perverse things. You will be like one who lies down in the midst of the sea, like one who lies on the top of a mast. "They struck me," you will say, "but I was not hurt; they beat me, but I did not feel it. When shall I awake? I must have another drink."

Proverbs 23:29-35, ESV

For the drunkard and the glutton shall come to poverty.

Proverbs 23:21, KJV

ANGER

Be not hasty in thy spirit to be angry: for anger resteth in the bosom of fools.

Ecclesiastes 7:9, KJV

There are times in life when anger can correct social and moral evils. And our society would be all the poorer if those who were moved to indignation did not act according to the dictates of their hearts. This kind of anger can be creative if the person experiencing it always keeps his goal in sight.

One of the consequences of unchanneled anger is that it easily rages out of control. When this happens, reason is supplanted by panic; planning by confusion. The vision of the greatness of life is reduced to the meanness and pettiness of the moment. The greatest tragedy of self-centered anger is that it separates you from God.

It is surprising how easily anger abates and balance returns to your life if God is at the center of your life. Uncontrolled anger can destroy your life, but the force of anger can become a righteous power if it is controlled by the Holy Spirit.

The Word's Angle

on Anger

Cain was very angry, and his face was downcast. Now Cain said to his brother Abel, "Let's go out to the field." And while they were in the field, Cain attacked his brother Abel and killed him.

Genesis 4:5, 8, NIV

Be ye angry, and sin not: let not the sun go down upon your wrath: Neither give place to the devil.

Ephesians 4:26-27, KJV

He that is slow to anger is better than the mighty.

Proverbs 16:32, KJV

Be angry, and do not sin; ponder in your own hearts on your beds, and be silent.

Psalm 4:4, ESV

Everyone should be quick to listen, slow to speak and slow to become angry, for man's anger does not bring about the righteous life that God desires.

James 1:19-20, NIV

Let all bitterness, wrath, anger, clamor, and evil speaking be put away from you, with all malice. And be kind to one another.

Ephesians 4:31-32, NKJV

Cease from anger, and forsake wrath; do not fret – it only causes harm.

Psalm 37:8, NKJV

"I tell you that anyone who is angry with his brother will be subject to judgment."

Matthew 5:22, NIV

But the meek shall inherit the earth; and shall delight themselves in the abundance of peace.

Psalm 37:11, KJV

Therefore, as the elect of God, holy and beloved, put on tender mercies, kindness, humility, meekness, longsuffering; bearing with one another, and forgiving one another.

Colossians 3:12-13, NKJV

Since, therefore, we have now been justified by his blood, much more shall we be saved by him from the wrath of God.

Romans 5:9, ESV

A soft answer turneth away wrath: but grievous words stir up anger.

Proverbs 15:1, KJV

The LORD is merciful and gracious, slow to anger and abounding in steadfast love.

Psalm 103:8, ESV

Love is patient, love is kind. It does not envy, it does not boast, it is not proud. It is not rude, it is not self-seeking, it is not easily angered, it keeps no record of wrongs.

1 Corinthians 13:4-5, NIV

A fool gives full vent to his spirit, but a wise man quietly holds it back.

Proverbs 29:11, ESV

Sing to the Lord, you saints of his; praise his holy name. For his anger lasts only a moment, but his favor lasts a lifetime.

Psalm 30:4-5, NIV

"For My name's sake I will defer My anger, and for My praise I will restrain it from you, so that I do not cut you off."

Isaiah 48:9, NKJV

$\mathcal{B}$URDENS

Praise be to the LORD, to God our Savior, who daily bears our burdens.

Psalm 68:19, NIV

Christ's promise to bear our burdens (Mt. 11:28) has brought strength to innumerable people. Many a pilgrim, weary of life's struggles, has derived new hope from it. To take your problems to Jesus and to find the peace that only He can give is one of the most enriching experiences we could have.

Unfortunately, people are often reluctant to let go of their burdens. They tell the Lord about all their worries, and then pick up their burden again and struggle on. Some people keep their burdens because they are so part of their lives, that they wouldn't know what to complain about without them.

Letting go of burdens is a gradual process. They need to be phased out of your life until they cease to exist. Ensure that you fill the void left by the vanished burdens with the indwelling Spirit of Christ. Then you will experience the peace that only Jesus, the Prince of Peace, can give you.

GOD'S PROMISES FOR

BURDEN ~ BEARERS

He says, "I removed the burden from their shoulders; their hands were set free from the basket. In your distress you called and I rescued you, I answered you out of a thundercloud."

Psalm 81:6-7, NIV

"Come to Me, all you who labor and are heavy laden, and I will give you rest. Take My yoke upon you and learn from Me, for I am gentle and lowly in heart, and you will find rest for your souls. For My yoke is easy and My burden is light."

Matthew 11:28-30, NKJV

For men are not cast off by the LORD forever. Though he brings grief, he will show compassion, so great is his unfailing love. For he does not willingly bring affliction or grief to the children of men.

Lamentations 3:31-33, NIV

Carry each other's burdens, and in this way you will fulfill the law of Christ.

Galatians 6:2, NIV

Cast thy burden upon the LORD, and he shall sustain thee: he shall never suffer the righteous to be moved.

Psalm 55:22, KJV

The LORD God is my strength; He will make my feet like deer's feet, and He will make me walk on my high hills.

Habakkuk 3:19, NKJV

And lest I should be exalted above measure through the abundance of theRevelations, there was given to me a thorn in the flesh, the messenger of Satan to buffet me, lest I should be exalted above measure. For this thing I besought the Lord thrice, that it might depart from me. And he said unto me, My grace is sufficient for thee: for my strength is made perfect in weakness. Most gladly therefore will I rather glory in my infirmities, that the power of Christ may rest upon me.

2 Corinthians 12:7-9, KJV

Surely he hath borne our griefs, and carried our sorrows: yet we did esteem him stricken, smitten of God, and afflicted.

Isaiah 53:4, KJV

Therefore we do not lose heart. Even though our outward man is perishing, yet the inward man is being renewed day by day. For our light affliction, which is but for a moment, is working for us a far more exceeding and eternal weight of glory.

2 Corinthians 4:16-17, NKJV

Many are the afflictions of the righteous, But the LORD delivers him out of them all.

Psalm 34:19, NKJV

We are afflicted in every way, but not crushed; perplexed, but not driven to despair.

2 Corinthians 4:8, ESV

The eternal God is thy refuge, and underneath are the everlasting arms.

Deuteronomy 33:27, KJV

COMFORT

May our Lord Jesus Christ Himself, and our God and Father, who has loved us and given us everlasting consolation and good hope by grace, comfort your hearts and establish you in every good word and work.

2 Thessalonians 2:16-17, NKJV

The apostle Paul encouraged Christians living in Philippi to turn their anxieties, which are robbers of peace, into prayers. They would then experience peace, he assured them, not a peace that the world knows but a peace that is the result of the Holy Spirit of God at work in their lives. Jesus promised peace to His disciples. Their security lay with Him. In the same way, Jesus wants to restore you to wholeness and peace, a life of new hope for the future.

Right now your greatest need is to experience quietness and rest in your spirit and healing from your grief. God's Holy Spirit is able to do that for you. It is only through His power that you can and will experience a deep, peaceful quieting of your riotous emotions.

The Word's Promises

of Comfort

"Blessed are those who mourn, For they shall be comforted."

Matthew 5:4, NKJV

But God, who comforts the downcast, comforted us by the coming of Titus, and not only by his coming but also by the comfort you had given him.

2 Corinthians 7:6-7, NIV

"I will pray the Father, and He will give you another Helper, that He may abide with you forever – the Spirit of truth, whom the world cannot receive, because it neither sees Him nor knows Him; but you know Him, for He dwells with you and will be in you. I will not leave you orphans; I will come to you."

John 14:16-18, NKJV

"But the Comforter, which is the Holy Ghost, whom the Father will send in my name, he shall teach you all things, and bring all things to your remembrance, whatsoever I have said unto you."

John 14:26, KJV

Thou shalt increase my greatness, and comfort me on every side.

Psalm 71:21, KJV

I have seen his ways, and will heal him: I will lead him also, and restore comforts unto him and to his mourners.

Isaiah 57:18, KJV

As one whom his mother comforts, so I will comfort you; you shall be comforted in Jerusalem.

Isaiah 66:13, ESV

"The Spirit of the Lord GOD is upon Me, because the LORD has anointed Me to preach good tidings to the poor; He has sent Me to heal the brokenhearted, to proclaim liberty to the captives, and the opening of the prison to those who are bound; to proclaim the acceptable year of the LORD, and the day of vengeance of our God; to comfort all who mourn."

Isaiah 61:1-2, NKJV

May your unfailing love be my comfort, according to your promise to your servant.

Psalm 119:76, NIV

For the LORD shall comfort Zion: he will comfort all her waste places; and he will make her wilderness like Eden, and her desert like the garden of the LORD; joy and gladness shall be found therein, thanksgiving, and the voice of melody.

Isaiah 51:3, KJV

Blessed be the God and Father of our Lord Jesus Christ, the Father of mercies and God of all comfort, who comforts us in all our tribulation, that we may be able to comfort those who are in any trouble, with the comfort with which we ourselves are comforted by God. For as the sufferings of Christ abound in us, so our consolation also abounds through Christ.

2 Corinthians 1:3-5, NKJV

Remember the word unto thy servant, upon which thou hast caused me to hope. This is my comfort in my affliction: for thy word hath quickened me. The proud have had me greatly in derision: yet have I not declined from thy law. I remembered thy judgments of old, O LORD; and have comforted myself.

Psalm 119:49-52, KJV

COURAGE

For God did not give us a spirit of timidity, but a spirit of power, of love and of self-discipline.
2 Timothy 1:7, NIV

We are never nearer to God than when we are troubled. We turn to Him, conscious of our own hopelessness and helplessness. And then, as we humble ourselves before Him, He fills us with His strength, His boldness, and His courage. The Bible admonishes us to be full of courage, because God knows that we can face every situation in life bravely. Not in our own strength and courage, but the power of God that Christ made available to us through His death and resurrection.

God promises us the courage to endure, the courage to overcome, the courage to be victorious, because we know that God is able to deliver us out of every difficulty that we find ourselves in. God is watching over us to keep us from harm, and to bring us safely to His eternal home.

Courage
from the Word

No, in all these things we are more than conquerors through him who loved us. For I am sure that neither death nor life, nor angels nor rulers, nor things present nor things to come, nor powers, nor height nor depth, nor anything else in all creation, will be able to separate us from the love of God in Christ Jesus our Lord.

Romans 8:37–39, ESV

"Have I not commanded you? Be strong and courageous. Do not be frightened, and do not be dismayed, for the LORD your God is with you wherever you go."

Joshua 1:9, ESV

Be strong and courageous. Do not be afraid or terrified because of them, for the LORD your God goes with you; he will never leave you nor forsake you.

Deuteronomy 31:6, NIV

Be watchful, stand firm in the faith, act like men, be strong.

1 Corinthians 16:13, ESV

Though I walk in the midst of trouble, you preserve my life; you stretch out your hand against the anger of my foes, with your right hand you save me.

Psalm 138:7, NIV

"These things I have spoken unto you, that in me ye might have peace. In the world ye shall have tribulation: but be of good cheer; I have overcome the world."

John 16:33, KJV

God is our refuge and strength, A very present help in trouble. Therefore we will not fear, even though the earth be removed, and though the mountains be carried into the midst of the sea.

Psalm 46:1-2, NKJV

He will cover you with his feathers, and under his wings you will find refuge; his faithfulness will be your shield and rampart. You will not fear the terror of night, nor the arrow that flies by day, nor the pestilence that stalks in the darkness, nor the plague that destroys at midday.

Psalm 91:4-6, NIV

The wicked flee when no man pursueth: but the righteous are bold as a lion.

Proverbs 28:1, KJV

In the fear of the LORD there is strong confidence, And His children will have a place of refuge.

Proverbs 14:26, NKJV

In him and through faith in him we may approach God with freedom and confidence.

Ephesians 3:12, NIV

Let us then with confidence draw near to the throne of grace, that we may receive mercy and find grace to help in time of need.

Hebrews 4:16, ESV

So we may boldly say: "The LORD is my helper; I will not fear. What can man do to me?"

Hebrews 13:6, NKJV

DEATH

Yea, though I walk through the valley of the shadow of death, I will fear no evil: for thou art with me; thy rod and thy staff they comfort me.

Psalm 23:4, KJV

The raising of Lazarus from the dead brings a powerful message to faithful Christians. It assures us that Jesus has ultimate power over life and death.

Paul saw death as a doorway into the eternal realm where God is. Death may be a frightening thought, but the assurance of eternal life ignites hope in our heavy hearts.

Christ has promised to return and bring with him every Christian who has "fallen asleep". We can look forward to the greatest reunion of all time, when all believers in Jesus, both dead and alive, will be united in heaven to enjoy fellowship with God forever. Heaven will be the final resting place of every Christian, free from death, sickness, suffering and pain ... forever.

Victory over

death

He will swallow up death forever; and the Lord GOD will wipe away tears from all faces, and the reproach of his people he will take away from all the earth, for the LORD has spoken.

Isaiah 25:8, ESV

He too shared in their humanity so that by his death he might destroy him who holds the power of death – that is, the devil – and free those who all their lives were held in slavery by their fear of death.

Hebrews 2:14-15, NIV

When the perishable puts on the imperishable, and the mortal puts on immortality, then shall come to pass the saying that is written: "Death is swallowed up in victory." "O death, where is your victory? O death, where is your sting?"

1 Corinthians 15:54-55, ESV

For I am convinced that neither death nor life, neither angels nor demons, neither the present nor the future, nor any powers, neither height nor depth, nor anything else in all creation, will be able to separate us from the love of God that is in Christ Jesus our Lord.

Romans 8:38-39, NIV

"Most assuredly, I say to you, if anyone keeps My word he shall never see death."

John 8:51, NKJV

For this God is our God for ever and ever: he will be our guide even unto death.

Psalm 48:14, KJV

"I am the Living One; I was dead, and behold I am alive for ever and ever! And I hold the keys of death and Hades."

Revelation 1:18, NIV

"For God so loved the world that He gave His only begotten Son, that whoever believes in Him should not perish but have everlasting life."

John 3:16, NKJV

For to me to live is Christ, and to die is gain.

Philippians 1:21, ESV

Jesus said unto her, I am the resurrection, and the life: he that believeth in me, though he were dead, yet shall he live: And whosoever liveth and believeth in me shall never die. Believest thou this?

John 11:25-26, KJV

Now if we died with Christ, we believe that we shall also live with Him, knowing that Christ, having been raised from the dead, dies no more. Death no longer has dominion over Him.

Romans 6:8-9, NKJV

If we live, we live to the Lord, and if we die, we die to the Lord. So then, whether we live or whether we die, we are the Lord's. For to this end Christ died and lived again, that he might be Lord both of the dead and of the living.

Romans 14:8-9, ESV

DEPRESSION

He heals the brokenhearted and binds up their wounds.

Psalm 147:3, ESV

In the life of each follower of Jesus Christ there will be dark days of depression and despair. Sometimes, for no apparent reason, doubt creeps into your heart. Your enthusiasm for the things of God is dampened, and your life seems to become mediocre.

This is often the result of a waning awareness of the presence of Christ in your life. You need a fresh experience with God to drive the darkness from your life. You need the awareness of His Holy Spirit to keep you from becoming insensitive.

In the darkness of doubt and depression you should cling to your faith in an unchanging God. No matter how your moods or spiritual feelings might fluctuate, God's love for you remains steadfast, strong, and secure. He loves you with an everlasting love and even though you may feel far from Him right now, remember that He is always close to you.

Dealing

with depression

"The Lord, He is the One who goes before you. He will be with you, He will not leave you nor forsake you; do not fear nor be dismayed."

Deuteronomy 31:8, NKJV

"I dwell in the high and holy place, with him who has a contrite and humble spirit, to revive the spirit of the humble, and to revive the heart of the contrite ones."

Isaiah 57:15, NKJV

The sacrifices of God are a broken spirit: a broken and a contrite heart, O God, thou wilt not despise.

Psalm 51:17, KJV

Why are you cast down, O my soul, and why are you in turmoil within me? Hope in God; for I shall again praise him, my salvation and my God.

Psalm 42:11, ESV

My heart is severely pained within me, and the terrors of death have fallen upon me. Fearfulness and trembling have come upon me, and horror has overwhelmed me. As for me, I will call upon God, and the LORD shall save me. Evening and morning and at noon I will pray, and cry aloud, and He shall hear my voice.

Psalm 55:4-5, 16-17, NKJV

"The Spirit of the LORD God is upon Me, because the LORD has anointed Me to preach good tidings to the poor; He has sent Me to heal the brokenhearted, to proclaim liberty to the captives, and the opening of the prison to those who are bound; to proclaim the acceptable year of the LORD, and the day of vengeance of our God; to comfort all who mourn."

Isaiah 61:1-2, NKJV

"Surely God does not reject a blameless man or strengthen the hands of evildoers. He will yet fill your mouth with laughter and your lips with shouts of joy."

Job 8:20-21, NIV

I waited patiently for the LORD; and he inclined unto me, and heard my cry. He brought me up also out of an horrible pit, out of the miry clay, and set my feet upon a rock, and established my goings. And he hath put a new song in my mouth, even praise unto our God: many shall see it, and fear, and shall trust in the LORD.

Psalm 40:1-3, KJV

"For the mountains may depart and the hills be removed, but my steadfast love shall not depart from you, and my covenant of peace shall not be removed," says the LORD.

Isaiah 54:10, ESV

The sorrows of death compassed me, and the floods of ungodly men made me afraid. The sorrows of hell compassed me about: the snares of death prevented me. In my distress I called upon the LORD, and cried unto my God: he heard my voice out of his temple, and my cry came before him, even into his ears.

Psalm 18:4-6, KJV

The LORD has comforted His people, and will have mercy on His afflicted.

Isaiah 49:13, NKJV

DIVORCE

If we confess our sins, he is faithful and just to forgive us our sins and to cleanse us from all unrighteousness.

1 *John* 1:9, ESV

It is widely accepted that divorce affects more than one third of all marriages, bringing with it the inevitable bruising experiences of failure, loss and grief. Major life changes such as the loss of custody of children, loss of status in the community, loss of financial security and loss of a common home will cause feelings of regret.

God's ideal is that a marriage should last a lifetime. It is not meant to break down. Yes, God does disapprove of divorce, but this does not mean He will not forgive the divorcée. We live in an imperfect world with imperfect people and when divorce occurs, God separates the sin from the sinner and continues to love him no matter what mistakes he may have made. Amazingly, God hurts when we are hurting, whether it is through our own fault or the failures of other people.

THE WORD'S VIEW

ON DIVORCE

The Lord God made a woman from the rib he had taken out of the man, and he brought her to the man. The man said, "This is now bone of my bones and flesh of my flesh; she shall be called 'woman,' for she was taken out of man." For this reason a man will leave his father and mother and be united to his wife, and they will become one flesh.

Genesis 2:22-24, NIV

He has not dealt with us according to our sins, nor punished us according to our iniquities. For as the heavens are high above the earth, so great is His mercy toward those who fear Him; as far as the east is from the west, so far has He removed our transgressions from us.

Psalm 103:10-12, NKJV

Marriage is honorable among all, and the bed undefiled; but fornicators and adulterers God will judge. Let your conduct be without covetousness; be content with such things as you have.

Hebrews 13:4-5, NKJV

You cover the LORD's altar with tears, with weeping and groaning because he no longer regards the offering or accepts it with favor from your hand. But you say, "Why does he not?" Because the LORD was witness between you and the wife of your youth, to whom you have been faithless, though she is your companion and your wife by covenant. Did he not make them one, with a portion of the Spirit in their union? And what was the one God seeking? Godly offspring. So guard yourselves in your spirit, and let none of you be faithless to the wife of youth. "For the man who hates and divorces, says the LORD, the God of Israel, covers his garment with violence, says the LORD of hosts. So guard yourselves in your spirit, and do not be faithless."

Malachi 2:13-16, ESV

And you, being dead in your sins and the uncircumcision of your flesh, hath he quickened together with him, having forgiven you all trespasses; Blotting out the handwriting of ordinances that was against us, which was contrary to us, and took it out of the way, nailing it to his cross.

Colossians 2:13-14, KJV

Some Pharisees came to him to test him. They asked, "Is it lawful for a man to divorce his wife for any and every reason?" "Haven't you read," he replied, "that at the beginning the Creator 'made them male and female,' and said, 'For this reason a man will leave his father and mother and be united to his wife, and the two will become one flesh'? So they are no longer two, but one. Therefore what God has joined together, let man not separate."

Matthew 19:3-6, NIV

I acknowledged my sin to you, and I did not cover my iniquity; I said, "I will confess my transgressions to the LORD," and you forgave the iniquity of my sin.

Psalm 32:5, ESV

"Come now, let us reason together," says the LORD. "Though your sins are like scarlet, they shall be as white as snow; though they are red as crimson, they shall be like wool."

Isaiah 1:18, NIV

$\mathcal{E}$VIL

Beloved, do not imitate evil but imitate good.
Whoever does good is from God; whoever does
evil has not seen God.

3 John 1:11, ESV

We don't have to look far to see the effects of evil in our world today. TV programs and movies sensationalize evil, newspapers make a living out of reporting on evil events, and magazines magnify the evil perpetrated in society. Sometimes it seems that the gates of hell are wide open and spewing forth all the wickedness that can be imagined.

Where is God when evil abounds? When wicked men seem to prosper and the righteous suffer? He still holds out His hands of love, ready to draw us into His presence. He still pours out His love to all who will receive it. He still proclaims His eternal goodness through the testimony of His children. And while evil seems to increase in a final attempt to overcome all that is good, we have God's eternal promise that the day will come when evil will be banished, the wicked will be punished, and the righteous will live forever in safety and peace.

GOD'S PROMISES OF
VICTORY OVER EVIL

Take no part in the unfruitful works of darkness, but instead expose them. For it is shameful even to speak of the things that they do in secret.

Ephesians 5:11-12, ESV

God is light, and in him is no darkness at all. If we say that we have fellowship with him, and walk in darkness, we lie, and do not the truth: But if we walk in the light, as he is in the light, we have fellowship one with another, and the blood of Jesus Christ his Son cleanseth us from all sin.

1 John 1:5-7, KJV

"And this is the judgment: the light has come into the world, and people loved the darkness rather than the light because their deeds were evil. For everyone who does wicked things hates the light and does not come to the light, lest his deeds should be exposed. But whoever does what is true comes to the light, so that it may be clearly seen that his deeds have been carried out in God."

John 3:19-21, ESV

Do not enter the path of the wicked, and do not walk in the way of evil. Avoid it, do not travel on it; turn away from it and pass on. For they do not sleep unless they have done evil; and their sleep is taken away unless they make someone fall. For they eat the bread of wickedness, and drink the wine of violence. But the path of the just is like the shining sun, that shines ever brighter unto the perfect day. The way of the wicked is like darkness; they do not know what makes them stumble.

Proverbs 4:14-19, NKJV

The mirth of the wicked is brief, the joy of the godless lasts but a moment.

Job 20:5, NIV

He who says he is in the light, and hates his brother, is in darkness until now. He who loves his brother abides in the light, and there is no cause for stumbling in him. But he who hates his brother is in darkness and walks in darkness, and does not know where he is going, because the darkness has blinded his eyes.

1 John 2:9-11, NKJV

Put on the full armor of God so that you can take your stand against the devil's schemes. For our struggle is not against flesh and blood, but against the rulers, against the authorities, against the powers of this dark world and against the spiritual forces of evil in the heavenly realms. Therefore put on the full armor of God, so that when the day of evil comes, you may be able to stand your ground, and after you have done everything, to stand.

Ephesians 6:11-13, NIV

He has delivered us from the domain of darkness and transferred us to the kingdom of his beloved Son.

Colossians 1:13, ESV

"I am come a light into the world, that whosoever believeth on me should not abide in darkness."

John 12:46, KJV

Again Jesus spoke to them, saying, "I am the light of the world. Whoever follows me will not walk in darkness, but will have the light of life."

John 8:12, ESV

$\mathcal{F}$EAR

*For God gave us a spirit not of fear but of power
and love and self-control.*

2 Timothy 1:7, ESV

I believe that people who say they are not ever
afraid either do not have sensitive spirits, or
they tend to hide the truth. If we succumb
to fear, our lives start disintegrating, our
thinking becomes chaotic, and our behavior
becomes reckless. That is why we need to
learn to control our fear.

It is important to prepare yourself in
times when you are not fearful for the times
when fear will encroach. To be afraid is a
natural reaction to many situations, and if
your spiritual resources are depleted when
it attacks, it could have serious consequences.

To overcome fear, you should yield
every area of your life to Christ. If Christ
controls your thinking and fills your spirit
with His Holy Spirit, you will, despite the
fear caused by circumstances, have inner
peace that is stronger than fear - even than
the fear of death.

FAITH

FOR THE FEARFUL

"Fear not, little flock; for it is your Father's good pleasure to give you the kingdom."

Luke 12:32, KJV

For I, the LORD your God, hold your right hand; it is I who say to you, "Fear not, I am the one who helps you."

Isaiah 41:13, ESV

He said to them, "Why are you so afraid? Have you still no faith?"

Mark 4:40, ESV

Do not be afraid of sudden terror, nor of trouble from the wicked when it comes; for the LORD will be your confidence, and will keep your foot from being caught.

Proverbs 3:25-26, NKJV

The LORD is my light and my salvation – whom shall I fear? The LORD is the stronghold of my life – of whom shall I be afraid?

Psalm 27:1, NIV

I, even I, am he that comforteth you: who art thou, that thou shouldest be afraid of a man that shall die, and of the son of man which shall be made as grass?

Isaiah 51:12, KJV

"Be strong and courageous. Do not be frightened, and do not be dismayed, for the LORD your God is with you wherever you go."

Joshua 1:9, ESV

He shall cover you with His feathers, and under His wings you shall take refuge; His truth shall be your shield and buckler. You shall not be afraid of the terror by night, nor of the arrow that flies by day, nor of the pestilence that walks in darkness, nor of the destruction that lays waste at noonday. A thousand may fall at your side, and ten thousand at your right hand; but it shall not come near you. No evil shall befall you, nor shall any plague come near your dwelling; for He shall give His angels charge over you, to keep you in all your ways. In their hands they shall bear you up, lest you dash your foot against a stone.

Psalm 91:4-7, 10-12, NKJV

He has said, "I will never leave you nor forsake you." So we can confidently say, "The Lord is my helper; I will not fear; what can man do to me?"

Hebrews 13:5-6, ESV

Fear not, for I have redeemed you; I have summoned you by name; you are mine. When you pass through the waters, I will be with you; and when you pass through the rivers, they will not sweep over you.

Isaiah 43:1-2, NIV

In God I have put my trust; I will not fear. What can flesh do to me?

Psalm 56:4, NKJV

"Be not afraid, only believe."

Mark 5:36, KJV

God is our refuge and strength, a very present help in trouble. Therefore we will not fear.

Psalm 46:1-2, NKJV

$\mathcal{F}$ORGIVENESS

If we confess our sins, he is faithful and just to forgive us our sins, and to cleanse us from all unrighteousness.

1 John 1:9, KJV

It is one of the great privileges and joys of the Christian faith that regardless of what you have done God is always waiting for you to come to Him in prayer. His love for you is so vast that you are assured of His forgiveness even before you enter into His presence. This assurance was given once and for all on Golgotha. All that you have to do is to turn in repentance to Christ and confess all your sins to Him.

There are two important matters that you need to consider. One is that God knows everything about you, including your weaknesses and shortcomings. The other is that despite it all He still loves you and always will. He gave His life to prove it.

Open your heart to Him and lay your guilt and fear before His throne of grace. Here you will experience the purifying balm of His unfathomable love.

GOD PROMISES

FORGIVENESS

I write unto you, little children, because your sins are forgiven you for his name's sake.

1 John 2:12, KJV

When we were overwhelmed by sins, you forgave our transgressions.

Psalm 65:2-3, NIV

I acknowledged my sin to you, and I did not cover my iniquity; I said, "I will confess my transgressions to the LORD," and you forgave the iniquity of my sin.

Psalm 32:5, ESV

I, even I, am he that blotteth out thy transgressions for mine own sake, and will not remember thy sins.

Isaiah 43:25, KJV

He has delivered us from the power of darkness and conveyed us into the kingdom of the Son of His love, in whom we have redemption through His blood, the forgiveness of sins.

Colossians 1:13-14, NKJV

In him we have redemption through his blood, the forgiveness of our trespasses, according to the riches of his grace, which he lavished upon us, in all wisdom and insight making known to us the mystery of his will, according to his purpose, which he set forth in Christ.

Ephesians 1:7-9, ESV

And you, being dead in your sins and the uncircumcision of your flesh, hath he quickened together with him, having forgiven you all trespasses; Blotting out the handwriting of ordinances that was against us, which was contrary to us, and took it out of the way, nailing it to his cross.

Colossians 2:13-14, KJV

He that covereth his sins shall not prosper: but whoso confesseth and forsaketh them shall have mercy.

Proverbs 28:13, KJV

"I have swept away your offenses like a cloud, your sins like the morning mist. Return to me, for I have redeemed you."

Isaiah 44:22, NIV

"Blessed are they whose transgressions are forgiven, whose sins are covered. Blessed is the man whose sin the Lord will never count against him."

Romans 4:7-8, NIV

And such were some of you. But you were washed, you were sanctified, you were justified in the name of the Lord Jesus Christ and by the Spirit of our God.

1 Corinthians 6:11, ESV

Come now, let us reason together, says the LORD: "Though your sins are like scarlet, they shall be as white as snow; though they are red like crimson, they shall become like wool."

Isaiah 1:18, ESV

All have sinned and fall short of the glory of God, and are justified freely by his grace through the redemption that came by Christ Jesus.

Romans 3:23-24, NIV

GRIEF

The LORD is close to the brokenhearted and saves those who are crushed in spirit.

Psalm 34:18, NIV

The Bible gives many examples of people who grieved deeply. Reading about their grief does not lessen our pain, but it helps to make us feel human, to understand that grief wounds us all at some time in life.

Jesus experienced intense grief in the garden of Gethsemane. His disciples lay asleep while he agonized over Judas' treacherous betrayal and His impending death. So deep was His grief that *"… his sweat was like blood"* (Lk. 22:44, NIV).

The Bible also tells us that when Jesus learned of the execution of John the Baptist, His cousin, He *"withdrew by boat to a solitary place"* (Mt. 14:13, NIV) to deal with His grief alone. He removed himself from the crowds which surrounded Him daily – He needed space to grieve, just as we all do.

Please remember that grief is a process. You must walk through the valley of tears, taking one step at a time.

COMFORT

FOR THE GRIEVING

The LORD upholdeth all that fall, and raiseth up all those that be bowed down.

Psalm 145:14, KJV

Those who sow in tears shall reap in joy.

Psalm 126:5, NKJV

He will swallow up death forever; and the Lord GOD will wipe away tears from all faces, and the reproach of his people he will take away from all the earth.

Isaiah 25:8, ESV

And the ransomed of the LORD shall return and come to Zion with singing; everlasting joy shall be upon their heads; they shall obtain gladness and joy, and sorrow and sighing shall flee away.

Isaiah 35:10, ESV

Sing, O heavens; and be joyful, O earth; and break forth into singing, O mountains: for the LORD hath comforted his people, and will have mercy upon his afflicted.

Isaiah 49:13, KJV

Mine eye is consumed because of grief; it waxeth old because of all mine enemies. Depart from me, all ye workers of iniquity; for the LORD hath heard the voice of my weeping. The LORD hath heard my supplication; the LORD will receive my prayer.

Psalm 6:7-9, KJV

Now may our Lord Jesus Christ Himself, and our God and Father, who has loved us and given us everlasting consolation and good hope by grace, comfort your hearts and establish you in every good word and work.

2 Thessalonians 2:16-17, NKJV

Hear, O LORD, and have mercy upon me: LORD, be thou my helper. Thou hast turned for me my mourning into dancing: thou hast put off my sackcloth, and girded me with gladness.

Psalm 30:10-11, KJV

God will wipe away every tear from their eyes; there shall be no more death, nor sorrow, nor crying. There shall be no more pain, for the former things have passed away.

Revelation 21:4, NKJV

"Blessed are they that mourn: for they shall be comforted."

Matthew 5:4, KJV

My life is consumed by anguish and my years by groaning; my strength fails because of my affliction, and my bones grow weak.

Psalm 31:10, NIV

Is there no balm in Gilead? Is there no physician there? Why then is there no healing for the wound of my people?

Jeremiah 8:22, NIV

Then he said to them, "My soul is overwhelmed with sorrow to the point of death. Stay here and keep watch with me."

Matthew 26:38, NIV

He is despised and rejected of men; a man of sorrows, and acquainted with grief: and we hid as it were our faces from him; he was despised, and we esteemed him not. Surely he hath borne our griefs, and carried our sorrows: yet we did esteem him stricken, smitten of God, and afflicted.

Isaiah 53:3-4, KJV

GRUDGES

*Forgive us our sins, for we also forgive everyone who
sins against us.*

Luke 11:4, NIV

If someone causes you hurt or suffering,
the natural reaction is to want to take
revenge. One of the most difficult demands
that Christianity places on us is to forgive
and forget. It is human nature to nurse a
grievance or harbor thoughts of revenge
until enmity is unleashed and relationships
are broken.

When you are hurt by an injustice, suffering undeserved pain, it is not easy to turn
the other cheek. Your natural reaction is
self-preservation. Forgiveness doesn't enter
your mind when you carry a grudge or try
to protect yourself from being hurt by
someone who has been insensitive.

To obey Christ's command to forgive is
not easy, but if the love of God is in your
heart, it is possible. Consider for a moment
the wonderful blessings you enjoy because
Jesus forgave you. Then you will not refuse
to forgive others.

Getting rid
of grudges

Strive for peace with everyone, and for the holiness without which no one will see the Lord. See to it that no one fails to obtain the grace of God; that no "root of bitterness" springs up and causes trouble, and by it many become defiled.

Hebrews 12:14-15, ESV

Love is patient, love is kind. It does not envy, it does not boast, it is not proud. It is not rude, it is not self-seeking, it is not easily angered, it keeps no record of wrongs.

1 Corinthians 13:4-5, NIV

You shall not take vengeance, nor bear any grudge against the children of your people, but you shall love your neighbor as yourself: I am the LORD.

Leviticus 19:18, NKJV

Confess your trespasses to one another, and pray for one another, that you may be healed.

James 5:16, NKJV

"If your brother sins, rebuke him, and if he repents, forgive him. If he sins against you seven times in a day, and seven times comes back to you and says, 'I repent,' forgive him."

Luke 17:3-4, NIV

For if ye forgive men their trespasses, your heavenly Father will also forgive you: But if ye forgive not men their trespasses, neither will your Father forgive your trespasses.

Matthew 6:14-15, KJV

Beloved, do not avenge yourselves, but rather give place to wrath; for it is written, "Vengeance is Mine, I will repay," says the Lord. Therefore "If your enemy is hungry, feed him; if he is thirsty, give him a drink; for in so doing you will heap coals of fire on his head."

Romans 12:19-20, NKJV

Be ye therefore merciful, as your Father also is merciful. Judge not, and ye shall not be judged: condemn not, and ye shall not be condemned: forgive, and ye shall be forgiven.

Luke 6:36-37, KJV

Be angry and do not sin; do not let the sun go down on your anger, and give no opportunity to the devil. Let all bitterness and wrath and anger and clamor and slander be put away from you, along with all malice. Be kind to one another, tenderhearted, forgiving one another, as God in Christ forgave you.

Ephesians 4:26-27, 31-32, ESV

"I say to you, love your enemies, bless those who curse you, do good to those who hate you, and pray for those who spitefully use you and persecute you, that you may be sons of your Father in heaven; for He makes His sun rise on the evil and on the good, and sends rain on the just and on the unjust. For if you love those who love you, what reward have you? Do not even the tax collectors do the same? And if you greet your brethren only, what do you do more than others? Do not even the tax collectors do so?"

Matthew 5:44-47, NKJV

"And whenever you stand praying, forgive, if you have anything against anyone, so that your Father also who is in heaven may forgive you your trespasses."

Mark 11:25, ESV

GUILT

For all have sinned, and come short of the glory of God.

Romans 3:23, KJV

Many people lead negative, miserable lives because they allow feelings of guilt to oppress them. They carry with them the burden of guilt over things in their past.

Scripture tells us very clearly that we are all sinners and that Jesus came to save sinners from their sin. His act of grace culminated in His crucifixion on Golgotha, where He sacrificed His life so that we can be forgiven.

If you are constantly haunted by guilt, it might be that you find it hard to truly believe that Christ died for you.

Free yourself from the chains of self-condemnation and guilt today. Turn to Christ with real remorse and true confession in your heart. Accept His redeeming grace with a grateful heart. Then you will be able to live a life of abundant grace.

Freedom from

GUILT

But we are all as an unclean thing, and all our righteousnesses are as filthy rags; and we all do fade as a leaf; and our iniquities, like the wind, have taken us away.

Isaiah 64:6, KJV

If we claim to be without sin, we deceive ourselves and the truth is not in us. If we confess our sins, he is faithful and just and will forgive us our sins and purify us from all unrighteousness.

1 John 1:8-9, NIV

O God, you know my folly; the wrongs I have done are not hidden from you. Let not those who hope in you be put to shame through me, let not those who seek you be brought to dishonor through me.

Psalm 69:5-6, ESV

For my iniquities have gone over my head; like a heavy burden, they are too heavy for me. Make haste to help me, O Lord, my salvation!

Psalm 38:4, 22, ESV

Then I acknowledged my sin to you and did not cover up my iniquity. I said, "I will confess my transgressions to the LORD" – and you forgave the guilt of my sin.

Psalm 32:5, NIV

Therefore let it be known to you, brethren, that through this Man is preached to you the forgiveness of sins; and by Him everyone who believes is justified from all things from which you could not be justified by the law of Moses.

Acts 13:38-39, NKJV

"'For I am merciful,' says the LORD; 'I will not remain angry forever. Only acknowledge your iniquity, that you have transgressed against the LORD your God.'"

Jeremiah 3:12-13, NKJV

He does not deal with us according to our sins, nor repay us according to our iniquities. For as high as the heavens are above the earth, so great is his steadfast love toward those who fear him; as far as the east is from the west, so far does he remove our transgressions from us.

Psalm 103:10-12, ESV

Have mercy upon me, O God, according to thy lovingkindness: according unto the multitude of thy tender mercies blot out my transgressions. Wash me throughly from mine iniquity, and cleanse me from my sin. For I acknowledge my transgressions: and my sin is ever before me. Against thee, thee only, have I sinned, and done this evil in thy sight: that thou mightest be justified when thou speakest, and be clear when thou judgest.

Psalm 51:1-4, KJV

Then one of the seraphs flew to me with a live coal in his hand, which he had taken with tongs from the altar. With it he touched my mouth and said, "See, this has touched your lips; your guilt is taken away and your sin atoned for."

Isaiah 6:6-7, NIV

And you, who were dead in your trespasses and the uncircumcision of your flesh, God made alive together with him, having forgiven us all our trespasses, by canceling the record of debt that stood against us with its legal demands. This he set aside, nailing it to the cross.

Colossians 2:13-14, ESV

$\mathcal{H}$ATRED

Hatred stirs up strife, but love covers all offenses.
Proverbs 10:12, ESV

It is true that one of the Master's most difficult commands is to love one another as He loves us. How can I love a cold-blooded murderer? How can I show love to someone who has harmed me?

In our own strength it is impossible, because human nature still clings to the principle of an eye for an eye and a tooth for a tooth. The only way to restore reason and stability to our world, is through the all-embracing, all-powerful love of God that can soften the hearts of the most hardened of men.

Jesus needs people who will display His love by praying for all people, regardless of how appalling their deeds may be. The Evil One has never had the power to conquer the power of prayer and love that comes in the Name of Christ. It is your privilege to be part of this miracle.

What the Word says

Thou shalt not hate thy brother in thine heart: thou shalt in any wise rebuke thy neighbour, and not suffer sin upon him. Thou shalt not avenge, nor bear any grudge against the children of thy people, but thou shalt love thy neighbour as thyself.

Leviticus 19:17-18, KJV

Anyone who claims to be in the light but hates his brother is still in the darkness. Whoever loves his brother lives in the light, and there is nothing in him to make him stumble. But whoever hates his brother is in the darkness and walks around in the darkness; he does not know where he is going, because the darkness has blinded him.

1 John 2:9-11, NIV

Put on then, as God's chosen ones, holy and beloved, compassion, kindness, humility, meekness, and patience, bearing with one another and, if one has a complaint against another, forgiving each other; as the LORD has forgiven you, so you also must forgive.

Colossians 3:12-13, ESV

If thine enemy be hungry, give him bread to eat; and if he be thirsty, give him water to drink.

Proverbs 25:21, KJV

"You have heard that it was said, 'Eye for eye, and tooth for tooth.' But I tell you, Do not resist an evil person. If someone strikes you on the right cheek, turn to him the other also. And if someone wants to sue you and take your tunic, let him have your cloak as well. If someone forces you to go one mile, go with him two miles. Give to the one who asks you, and do not turn away from the one who wants to borrow from you."

Matthew 5:38-42, NIV

"A new commandment I give to you, that you love one another; as I have loved you, that you also love one another. By this all will know that you are My disciples, if you have love for one another."

John 13:34-35, NKJV

Let love be genuine. Abhor what is evil; hold fast to what is good. Love one another with brotherly affection. Outdo one another in showing honor.

Romans 12:9-10, ESV

Beloved, let us love one another: for love is of God; and every one that loveth is born of God, and knoweth God. He that loveth not knoweth not God; for God is love. Beloved, if God so loved us, we ought also to love one another.

1 John 4:7-8, 11, KJV

He who hates, disguises it with his lips, and lays up deceit within himself; when he speaks kindly, do not believe him, for there are seven abominations in his heart; though his hatred is covered by deceit, his wickedness will be revealed before the assembly.

Proverbs 26:24-26, NKJV

"But love ye your enemies, and do good, and lend, hoping for nothing again; and your reward shall be great, and ye shall be the children of the Highest: for he is kind unto the unthankful and to the evil."

Luke 6:35, KJV

"You have heard that it was said, 'You shall love your neighbor and hate your enemy.' But I say to you, Love your enemies and pray for those who persecute you."

Matthew 5:43-44, ESV

HEALING

"See now that I myself am He! There is no god besides me. I put to death and I bring to life, I have wounded and I will heal, and no one can deliver out of my hand."

Deuteronomy 32:39, NIV

Few things are as devastating as prolonged ill health. It undermines our physical strength, drains us emotionally, and depletes our spiritual resources. Sometimes illnesses are a result of our own negligence but sometimes they just seem to come upon us, no matter how carefully we live. The truth is that our bodies are subject to decay, and in this world we will suffer sickness and pain.

God cares about our physical condition, just as He cares about our spiritual condition. Therefore, we can ask God to touch us in our illnesses, but understanding too, that healing does not always occur in dramatic ways. Sometimes it is a slow process of recovery that gives the patient time to pray and focus on spiritual well-being. Sometimes there is a deterioration and even death. But, remember, death is simply a doorway to eternal health and wholeness!

THE WORD'S VIEW

ON HEALING

He sent out his word and healed them, and delivered them from their destruction. Let them thank the LORD for his steadfast love, for his wondrous works to the children of men!

Psalm 107:20-21, ESV

Surely he hath borne our griefs, and carried our sorrows: yet we did esteem him stricken, smitten of God, and afflicted. But he was wounded for our transgressions, he was bruised for our iniquities: the chastisement of our peace was upon him; and with his stripes we are healed.

Isaiah 53:4-5, KJV

Many who were demon-possessed were brought to him, and he drove out the spirits with a word and healed all the sick. This was to fulfill what was spoken through the prophet Isaiah: "He took up our infirmities and carried our diseases."

Matthew 8:16-17, NIV

Bless the LORD, O my soul, and forget not all his benefits: Who forgiveth all thine iniquities; who healeth all thy diseases.

Psalm 103:2-3, KJV

Heal me, O LORD, and I shall be healed; save me, and I shall be saved: for thou art my praise.

Jeremiah 17:14, KJV

"So you shall serve the LORD your God, and He will bless your bread and your water. And I will take sickness away from the midst of you."

Exodus 23:25, NKJV

For I will restore health unto thee, and I will heal thee of thy wounds, saith the LORD.

Jeremiah 30:17, KJV

Blessed is he that considereth the poor: the LORD will deliver him in time of trouble. The LORD will preserve him, and keep him alive; and he shall be blessed upon the earth: and thou wilt not deliver him unto the will of his enemies. The LORD will strengthen him upon the bed of languishing: thou wilt make all his bed in his sickness.

Psalm 41:1-3, KJV

Is anyone among you sick? Let him call for the elders of the church, and let them pray over him, anointing him with oil in the name of the Lord. And the prayer of faith will save the one who is sick, and the Lord will raise him up. And if he has committed sins, he will be forgiven. Therefore, confess your sins to one another and pray for one another, that you may be healed. The prayer of a righteous person has great power as it is working.

James 5:14-16, ESV

He himself bore our sins in his body on the tree, so that we might die to sins and live for righteousness; by his wounds you have been healed.

1 Peter 2:24, NKJV

His fame went throughout all Syria; and they brought to Him all sick people who were afflicted with various diseases and torments, and those who were demon-possessed, epileptics, and paralytics; and He healed them.

Matthew 4:24, NKJV

$\mathcal{H}$EAVEN

Our citizenship is in heaven, from which we also eagerly wait for the Savior, the Lord Jesus Christ.
Philippians 3:20, NKJV

C.S. Lewis noted that Christians who have a firm conviction of the reality of heaven are the happiest people on earth. Heaven is a very real place, and an essential doctrine of the Gospel of Christ. Christ died so that we might live with Him forever – in Heaven! And He comforted His disciples before His death with the assurance of a place that He would prepare for them. He is preparing a place for us, too. And He will come and take us to that place, whether through death or His Second Coming. Then all the heartache and pain of this world will be forgotten forever. He will wipe away every tear, and every wound – whether physical or emotional – that we have ever received, will be healed.

The promise of heaven sustains us when we suffer the hurts of this world. For in that promise is the assurance of joy and life overflowing with goodness for evermore.

THE WORD'S PROMISES

OF HEAVEN

"Verily, verily, I say unto thee, Except a man be born of water and of the Spirit, he cannot enter into the kingdom of God."

John 3:5, KJV

"In my Father's house are many rooms; if it were not so, I would have told you. I am going there to prepare a place for you. And if I go and prepare a place for you, I will come back and take you to be with me that you also may be where I am."

John 14:2-3, NIV

"Not every one that saith unto me, Lord, Lord, shall enter into the kingdom of heaven; but he that doeth the will of my Father which is in heaven."

Matthew 7:21, KJV

"Store up for yourselves treasures in heaven, where moth and rust do not destroy, and where thieves do not break in and steal. For where your treasure is, there your heart will be also."

Matthew 6:20-21, NIV

And said, Verily I say unto you, Except ye be converted, and become as little children, ye shall not enter into the kingdom of heaven. Whosoever therefore shall humble himself as this little child, the same is greatest in the kingdom of heaven.

Matthew 18:3-4, KJV

"The kingdom of heaven is like treasure hidden in a field, which a man found and covered up. Then in his joy he goes and sells all that he has and buys that field. Again, the kingdom of heaven is like a merchant in search of fine pearls, who, on finding one pearl of great value, went and sold all that he had and bought it. Again, the kingdom of heaven is like a net that was thrown into the sea and gathered fish of every kind. When it was full, men drew it ashore and sat down and sorted the good into containers but threw away the bad. So it will be at the close of the age. The angels will come out and separate the evil from the righteous and throw them into the fiery furnace. In that place there will be weeping and gnashing of teeth."

Matthew 13:44-50, ESV

"Nevertheless do not rejoice in this, that the spirits are subject to you, but rather rejoice because your names are written in heaven."

Luke 10:20, NKJV

Now we know that if the earthly tent we live in is destroyed, we have a building from God, an eternal house in heaven, not built by human hands. Meanwhile we groan, longing to be clothed with our heavenly dwelling.

2 Corinthians 5:1-2, NIV

But according to his promise we are waiting for new heavens and a new earth in which righteousness dwells.

2 Peter 3:13, ESV

"For behold, I create new heavens and a new earth; and the former shall not be remembered or come to mind."

Isaiah 65:17, NKJV

And God shall wipe away all tears from their eyes; and there shall be no more death, neither sorrow, nor crying, neither shall there be any more pain: for the former things are passed away.

Revelation 21:4, KJV

$\mathcal{H}$OPELESSNESS

We have put our hope in the living God, who is the Savior of all men, and especially of those who believe.

1 Timothy 4:10, NIV

There are times when everything seems as dark as night and the future appears bleak and grim. In these days of unrest, anarchy, and crime, with an uncertain economy, with famines and earthquakes, wars and rumors of war it seems that all is not well. Yet, above our pessimism, above our oppressive circumstances, above the clamor of dark forces, the voice of Jesus is heard – clear, triumphant and liberating: *"Take heart! I have overcome the world"* (Jn. 16:33, NIV).

No matter how hopeless things appear, the Christian always sets his hope in Christ. In spite of all that Jesus faced, He rose victorious over death in the darkest hour in the history of mankind. He conquered the grave and death when He transformed the darkness of Golgotha into the light of the resurrection. And He can turn your darkness into light too.

Hope for

THE HOPELESS

Behold, the eye of the LORD is on those who fear him, on those who hope in his steadfast love, that he may deliver their soul from death and keep them alive in famine. Our soul waits for the LORD; he is our help and our shield.

Psalm 33:18-20, ESV

Thou art my hiding place and my shield: I hope in thy word.

Psalm 119:114, KJV

I waited patiently for the LORD; and he inclined unto me, and heard my cry. He brought me up also out of an horrible pit, out of the miry clay, and set my feet upon a rock, and established my goings. And he hath put a new song in my mouth, even praise unto our God: many shall see it, and fear, and shall trust in the LORD.

Psalm 40:1-3, KJV

And every man that hath this hope in him purifieth himself, even as he is pure.

1 John 3:3, KJV

Show me your ways, O Lord, teach me your paths; guide me in your truth and teach me, for you are God my Savior, and my hope is in you all day long.

Psalm 25:4-5, NIV

May the God of hope fill you with all joy and peace in believing, so that by the power of the Holy Spirit you may abound in hope.

Romans 15:13, ESV

Those who hope in the Lord will renew their strength. They will soar on wings like eagles; they will run and not grow weary, they will walk and not be faint.

Isaiah 40:31, NIV

Therefore did my heart rejoice, and my tongue was glad; moreover also my flesh shall rest in hope: Because thou wilt not leave my soul in hell, neither wilt thou suffer thine Holy One to see corruption.

Acts 2:26-27, KJV

Therefore gird up the loins of your mind, be sober, and rest your hope fully upon the grace that is to be brought to you at the Revelation of Jesus Christ.

1 Peter 1:13, NKJV

Uphold me according unto thy word, that I may live: and let me not be ashamed of my hope.

Psalm 119:116, KJV

For thus says the High and Lofty One who inhabits eternity, whose name is Holy: "I dwell in the high and holy place, with him who has a contrite and humble spirit, to revive the spirit of the humble, and to revive the heart of the contrite ones."

Isaiah 57:15, NKJV

Be strong, and let your heart take courage, all you who wait for the LORD!

Psalm 31:24, ESV

Thus says the LORD: "Cursed is the man who trusts in man and makes flesh his strength, whose heart turns away from the LORD. He is like a shrub in the desert, and shall not see any good come. He shall dwell in the parched places of the wilderness, in an uninhabited salt land. Blessed is the man who trusts in the LORD, whose trust is the LORD."

Jeremiah 17:5-7, ESV

INJUSTICE

"And will not God give justice to his elect, who cry to him day and night? Will he delay long over them? I tell you, he will give justice to them speedily."
Luke 18:7-8, ESV

Few things rile good people more than injustice – the poor who are oppressed, the weak who are tormented, the good who are unjustly accused all rouse our sympathy and compassion. Even the justice systems of most countries seem to favor the wicked, if their pockets are deep enough. And the cry of the righteous still echoes through the centuries: *"How long, O LORD, will the wicked be jubilant?"* (Ps. 94:3, NIV).

The good news of the gospel is that Christ came to set the prisoners free, to proclaim the day of the vengeance of our God. The wicked will not prosper forever. They will stand before the just God of the universe, and they will receive the justice they deserve. We do what we can here and now to eradicate injustice around us, knowing that justice and righteousness will triumph, because our God holds the scepter of justice in His hand.

THE WORD'S VIEW

ON INJUSTICE

The lip of truth shall be established for ever: but a lying tongue is but for a moment.

Proverbs 12:19, KJV

Let God be true, and every man a liar. As it is written: "So that you may be proved right when you speak and prevail when you judge."

Romans 3:4, NIV

For the Lord GOD will help me; therefore shall I not be confounded: therefore have I set my face like a flint, and I know that I shall not be ashamed. He is near that justifieth me; who will contend with me? let us stand together: who is mine adversary? let him come near to me. Behold, the Lord GOD will help me; who is he that shall condemn me? lo, they all shall wax old as a garment; the moth shall eat them up.

Isaiah 50:7-9, KJV

We know him who said, "It is mine to avenge; I will repay," and again, "The Lord will judge his people." It is a dreadful thing to fall into the hands of the living God.

Hebrews 10:30-31, NKJV

For this is thankworthy, if a man for conscience toward God endure grief, suffering wrongfully. For what glory is it, if, when ye be buffeted for your faults, ye shall take it patiently? but if, when ye do well, and suffer for it, ye take it patiently, this is acceptable with God. For even hereunto were ye called: because Christ also suffered for us, leaving us an example, that ye should follow his steps.

1 Peter 2:19-21, KJV

"If the world hates you, know that it has hated me before it hated you. If you were of the world, the world would love you as its own; but because you are not of the world, but I chose you out of the world, therefore the world hates you."

John 15:18-19, ESV

The LORD executeth righteousness and judgment for all that are oppressed.

Psalm 103:6, KJV

You prepare a table before me in the presence of my enemies. You anoint my head with oil; my cup overflows. Surely goodness and love will follow me all the days of my life, and I will dwell in the house of the LORD forever.

Psalm 23:5-6, NIV

Who shall lay any thing to the charge of God's elect? It is God that justifieth. Who is he that condemneth? It is Christ that died, yea rather, that is risen again, who is even at the right hand of God, who also maketh intercession for us.

Romans 8:33-34, KJV

"All who rage against you will surely be ashamed and disgraced; those who oppose you will be as nothing and perish. Though you search for your enemies, you will not find them. Those who wage war against you will be as nothing at all. For I am the LORD, your God, who takes hold of your right hand and says to you, Do not fear; I will help you."

Isaiah 41:11-13, NIV

$\mathcal{J}$EALOUSY

A heart at peace gives life to the body, but envy rots the bones.

Proverbs 14:30, NIV

There are two kinds of envy. The one comprises desire for the possessions of others. This envy is difficult to control because it is such a typical human weakness. The other kind is much worse: it resents the fact that other people have that which you do not have. This jealousy does not so much imply that we would like other people's possessions, but rather that we begrudge those who possess something. Meanness of the soul cannot sink much lower than that.

If the believer succumbs to his sinful nature and does not allow himself to be guided by the Holy Spirit, all kinds of practices of this sinful nature will come to the fore: hostility, hatred, jealousy, rage, discord, disagreement, rifts and envy. The only remedy for this is love that "does not envy", but that accepts things as God has planned them for this life.

The Word's view

on jealousy

You shall not set your desire on your neighbor's house or land, his manservant or maidservant, his ox or donkey, or anything that belongs to your neighbor.

Deuteronomy 5:21, NIV

Wrath is cruel and anger a torrent, but who is able to stand before jealousy?

Proverbs 27:4, NKJV

Let us walk honestly, as in the day; not in rioting and drunkenness, not in chambering and wantonness, not in strife and envying.

Romans 13:13, KJV

"What comes out of a man, that defiles a man. For from within, out of the heart of men, proceed evil thoughts, adulteries, fornications, murders, thefts, covetousness, wickedness, deceit, lewdness, an evil eye, blasphemy, pride, foolishness. All these evil things come from within and defile a man."

Mark 7:20-23, NKJV

So put away all malice and all deceit and hypocrisy and envy and all slander.

1 Peter 2:1, ESV

Let not thine heart envy sinners: but be thou in the fear of the LORD all the day long.

Proverbs 23:17, KJV

Those who are Christ's have crucified the flesh with its passions and desires. If we live in the Spirit, let us also walk in the Spirit. Let us not become conceited, provoking one another, envying one another.

Galatians 5:24-26, NKJV

Who is wise and understanding among you? Let him show it by his good life, by deeds done in the humility that comes from wisdom. But if you harbor bitter envy and selfish ambition in your hearts, do not boast about it or deny the truth. Such "wisdom" does not come down from heaven but is earthly, unspiritual, of the devil. For where you have envy and selfish ambition, there you find disorder and every evil practice.

James 3:13-16, NIV

Let no one seek his own good, but the good of his neighbor.

1 Corinthians 10:24, ESV

Godliness with contentment is great gain. For we brought nothing into the world, and we can take nothing out of it. But if we have food and clothing, we will be content with that.

1 Timothy 6:6-8, NIV

Better is a handful of quietness than two hands full of toil and a striving after wind.

Ecclesiastes 4:6, ESV

Rest in the LORD, and wait patiently for Him; do not fret because of him who prospers in his way, because of the man who brings wicked schemes to pass. For evildoers shall be cut off; but those who wait on the LORD, they shall inherit the earth.

Psalm 37:7, 9, NKJV

For wrath killeth the foolish man, and envy slayeth the silly one.

Job 5:2, KJV

$\mathcal{J}$OY

You will show me the path of life; in Your presence is fullness of joy; at Your right hand are pleasures forevermore.

Psalm 16:11, NKJV

Christ's happiness, blessing and joy are indestructible (see Jn. 16:22). Christ's happiness is a blessing, even when we are in pain. It is a joy that cannot be erased by sorrow, loss, disappointment, or failure. It is a happiness that sees a rainbow through your tears. It is something that nothing in life or death can deprive us of.

Christ's happiness does not necessarily coincide with our external circumstances. It is a deep joy that is everlasting and steadfast. It is not a human feat that we achieve through our own effort. It is a gift of God in our lives, through the work of the Holy Spirit. The Holy Spirit will guide us to be obedient to Christ, so that His happiness and blessing will become our portion. Pray that the Holy Spirit will clearly lead us and that He will inspire us so that we will yearn for the "happiness" and "blessing" of Christ.

Joy from
the Word

"Until now you have asked nothing in My name. Ask, and you will receive, that your joy may be full."

John 16:24, NKJV

Be glad in the LORD, and rejoice, ye righteous: and shout for joy, all ye that are upright in heart.

Psalm 32:11, KJV

We also rejoice in God through our Lord Jesus Christ, through whom we have now received the reconciliation.

Romans 5:11, NKJV

"These things have I spoken unto you, that my joy might remain in you, and that your joy might be full."

John 15:11, KJV

For you, O LORD, have made me glad by your work; at the works of your hands I sing for joy.

Psalm 92:4, ESV

For the kingdom of God is not a matter of eating and drinking but of righteousness and peace and joy in the Holy Spirit.

Romans 14:17, ESV

"Blessed are you when they revile and persecute you, and say all kinds of evil against you falsely for My sake. Rejoice and be exceedingly glad, for great is your reward in heaven, for so they persecuted the prophets who were before you."

Matthew 5:11-12, NKJV

We also rejoice in our sufferings, because we know that suffering produces perseverance; perseverance, character; and character, hope.

Romans 5:3-4, NIV

Make a joyful noise to the LORD, all the earth! Serve the LORD with gladness! Come into his presence with singing!

Psalm 100:1-2, ESV

Burst into songs of joy together, you ruins of Jerusalem, for the LORD has comforted his people, he has redeemed Jerusalem.

Isaiah 52:9, NIV

JOY

O sing unto the LORD a new song; for he hath done marvellous things: his right hand, and his holy arm, hath gotten him the victory. Make a joyful noise unto the LORD, all the earth: make a loud noise, and rejoice, and sing praise. Sing unto the LORD with the harp; with the harp, and the voice of a Psalm.

Psalm 98:1, 4-5, KJV

Now you do not see Him, yet believing, you rejoice with joy inexpressible and full of glory, receiving the end of your faith – the salvation of your souls.

1 Peter 1:8-9, NKJV

You turned my wailing into dancing; you removed my sackcloth and clothed me with joy, that my heart may sing to you and not be silent. O LORD my God, I will give you thanks forever.

Psalm 30:11-12, NIV

They that sow in tears shall reap in joy. He that goeth forth and weepeth, bearing precious seed, shall doubtless come again with rejoicing, bringing his sheaves with him.

Psalm 126:5-6, KJV

$\mathcal{L}$ONELINESS

Turn to me and be gracious to me, for I am lonely and afflicted.

Psalm 25:16, ESV

There are many people who feel that they have no one to turn to, and there are others who claim that they have no family. But through Jesus you can be part of the most privileged family on earth: the family of God.

Your surrender to the Lord Jesus opened the door to the love and concern of the almighty God who is also your heavenly Father. Through Christ you too are invited to become a child of God, and as such to enjoy the loving relationship that exists between Parent and child. This is an everlasting relationship, because the Lord has promised to be with you always and never to forsake you (see Heb. 23:5).

If you turn to Jesus in all circumstances and place your trust in Him completely, you will experience the protective love of God that will grant you the peace that transcends all understanding. And then you will never again feel as if you are alone in life.

COMFORT

FOR THE LONELY

Even my close friend in whom I trusted, who ate my bread, has lifted his heel against me. But you have upheld me because of my integrity, and set me in your presence forever.

Psalm 41:9, 12, ESV

No one came to my support, but everyone deserted me. May it not be held against them. But the Lord stood at my side and gave me strength.

2 Timothy 4:16-17, NIV

"I will pray the Father, and He will give you another Helper, that He may abide with you forever – the Spirit of truth, whom the world cannot receive, because it neither sees Him nor knows Him; but you know Him, for He dwells with you and will be in you. I will not leave you orphans; I will come to you."

John 14:16-18, NKJV

"I am with you always, even to the end of the age."

Matthew 28:20, NKJV

A father of the fatherless, and a judge of the widows, is God in his holy habitation. God setteth the solitary in families: he bringeth out those which are bound with chains: but the rebellious dwell in a dry land.

Psalm 68:5-6, KJV

The LORD is good to those who wait for him, to the soul who seeks him.

Lamentations 3:25, ESV

"Can a mother forget the baby at her breast and have no compassion on the child she has borne? Though she may forget, I will not forget you! See, I have engraved you on the palms of my hands; your walls are ever before me."

Isaiah 49:15-16, NIV

And my God will supply every need of yours according to his riches in glory in Christ Jesus.

Philippians 4:19, ESV

"As I was with Moses, so I will be with you. I will not leave you nor forsake you."

Joshua 1:5, NKJV

You will call, and the LORD will answer; you will cry for help, and he will say: Here am I.

Isaiah 58:9, NIV

So we, though many, are one body in Christ, and individually members one of another.

Romans 12:5, ESV

When my father and my mother forsake me, then the LORD will take care of me.

Psalm 27:10, NKJV

I am with thee, and will keep thee in all places whither thou goest ... I will not leave thee, until I have done that which I have spoken to thee of.

Genesis 28:15, KJV

The LORD himself goes before you and will be with you; he will never leave you nor forsake you.

Deuteronomy 31:8, NIV

Draw near to God, and he will draw near to you.

James 4:8, ESV

$\mathcal{L}$OVE

In this is love, not that we loved God, but that He loved us and sent His Son to be the propitiation for our sins. Beloved, if God so loved us, we also ought to love one another.

1 John 4:10–11, NKJV

God is love. It is not only that He loves us but that He *is* love. This means that the cause of His loving us is found in Himself and not in us, and for that reason His love is changeless.

God is love and He loves us apart from our response so that His love does not fluctuate with our fickle nature.

His heart is disposed to us in love; He is rich in mercy; He first loved us. The result is that he commended His love to us, in that when we were rebellious He gave His own Son for us, and planned our restoration, our acceptance, our enthronement. A God who loves and gives like that will surely provide all things that we need, and there is only one thing we can do in return, namely to love Him.

GOD'S PROMISES

OF LOVE

The LORD hath appeared of old unto me, saying, Yea, I have loved thee with an everlasting love: therefore with lovingkindness have I drawn thee.

Jeremiah 31:3, KJV

Give thanks to the LORD, for he is good; his love endures forever.

1 Chronicles 16:34, NIV

Hereby perceive we the love of God, because he laid down his life for us: and we ought to lay down our lives for the brethren.

1 John 3:16, KJV

Your steadfast love, O LORD, extends to the heavens, your faithfulness to the clouds. How precious is your steadfast love, O God! The children of mankind take refuge in the shadow of your wings.

Psalm 36:5, 7, ESV

The LORD is gracious and merciful, slow to anger and abounding in steadfast love.

Psalm 145:8, ESV

"God so loved the world that He gave His only begotten Son, that whoever believes in Him should not perish but have everlasting life."

John 3:16, NKJV

"Though the mountains be shaken and the hills be removed, yet my unfailing love for you will not be shaken nor my covenant of peace be removed," says the LORD, who has compassion on you.

Isaiah 54:10, NIV

For I am persuaded, that neither death, nor life, nor angels, nor principalities, nor powers, nor things present, nor things to come, Nor height, nor depth, nor any other creature, shall be able to separate us from the love of God, which is in Christ Jesus our Lord.

Romans 8:38-39, KJV

Dear friends, let us love one another, for love comes from God. Everyone who loves has been born of God and knows God. Whoever does not love does not know God, because God is love.

1 John 4:7-8, NIV

LOVE

See what kind of love the Father has given to us, that we should be called children of God; and so we are.

1 John 3:1, ESV

May the Lord make your love increase and overflow for each other and for everyone else.

1 Thessalonians 3:12, NIV

Walk in love, as Christ also has loved us and given Himself for us, an offering and a sacrifice to God for a sweet-smelling aroma.

Ephesians 5:2, NKJV

If I speak in the tongues of men and of angels, but have not love, I am a noisy gong or a clanging cymbal. Love is patient and kind; love does not envy or boast; it is not arrogant or rude. It does not insist on its own way; it is not irritable or resentful; it does not rejoice at wrongdoing, but rejoices with the truth. Love bears all things, believes all things, hopes all things, endures all things. Love never ends.

1 Corinthians 13:1, 4-8, ESV

$\mathcal{P}$OVERTY

He raises the poor out of the dust, and lifts the
needy out of the ash heap, that He may seat him
with princes – with the princes of His people.

Psalm 113:7-8, NKJV

Many people are unaware of the immeasurable generosity of God. Their own needs and dire poverty blind them and separate them from the One who could ease their suffering and transform their poverty into luxury.

Scripture reveals to us the joyful fact that God is much more willing to give than we are to receive. If we would only pray and believe sincerely and in faith, we could receive that which we pray for. Many disciples want to believe unconditionally and yet there are few who utilize the key which God makes available to unlock His abundance.

If you bring a request to your heavenly Father, make sure you don't harbor doubt. Such an attitude creates distrust; prayers are not answered until doubt is replaced by faith. God hears your prayers and will meet your every need from His treasure house – according to His glorious grace.

The Word's view

on poverty

"Bring the whole tithe into the storehouse, that there may be food in my house. Test me in this," says the Lord Almighty, "and see if I will not throw open the floodgates of heaven and pour out so much blessing that you will not have room enough for it."

Malachi 3:10, NIV

For I was envious of the boastful, when I saw the prosperity of the wicked. Their eyes bulge with abundance; they have more than heart could wish. When I thought how to understand this, it was too painful for me – until I went into the sanctuary of God; then I understood their end. Those who are far from You shall perish.

Psalm 73:3, 7, 16-17, 27, NKJV

They that trust in their wealth, and boast themselves in the multitude of their riches; none of them can by any means redeem his brother, nor give to God a ransom for him.

Psalm 49:6-7, KJV

Command those who are rich in this present world not to be arrogant nor to put their hope in wealth, which is so uncertain, but to put their hope in God, who richly provides us with everything for our enjoyment. Command them to do good, to be rich in good deeds, and to be generous and willing to share.

1 Timothy 6:17-18, NIV

Defend the poor and fatherless: do justice to the afflicted and needy. Deliver the poor and needy: rid them out of the hand of the wicked.

Psalm 82:3-4, KJV

The LORD maketh poor, and maketh rich: he bringeth low, and lifteth up. He raiseth up the poor out of the dust, and lifteth up the beggar from the dunghill, to set them among princes, and to make them inherit the throne of glory: for the pillars of the earth are the LORD's, and he hath set the world upon them.

1 Samuel 2:7-8, KJV

This poor man called, and the LORD heard him; he saved him out of all his troubles.

Psalm 34:6, NIV

For thou hast been a strength to the poor, a strength to the needy in his distress, a refuge from the storm, a shadow from the heat, when the blast of the terrible ones is as a storm against the wall.

Isaiah 25:4, KJV

He will bring justice to the poor of the people; he will save the children of the needy.

Psalm 72:4, NKJV

"Because the poor are plundered, because the needy groan, I will now arise," says the LORD; "I will place him in the safety for which he longs."

Psalm 12:5, ESV

"The poor and needy search for water, but there is none; their tongues are parched with thirst. But I the LORD will answer them; I, the God of Israel, will not forsake them."

Isaiah 41:17, NIV

I am poor and needy; yet the LORD thinks upon me. You are my help and my deliverer; do not delay, O my God.

Psalm 40:17, NKJV

$\mathscr{P}$RAYER

Evening, and morning, and at noon, will I pray, and cry aloud: and he shall hear my voice.

Psalm 55:17, KJV

God shapes the world by prayers. The lips that uttered them may have closed in death, the heart that felt them may have ceased to beat, but the prayers outlive the lives of an age, outlive a world. That man is most immortal who has done the most and best praying. They are God's heroes, God's saints, God's servants. The prayers of God's saints are the capital stock in Heaven by which Christ carries on His great work on earth. Earth is changed, revolutionized, angels move on more powerful, more rapid wings, and God's policy is shaped as the prayers are more numerous, more efficient. It is true that the mightiest successes that come to God's cause are created and carried on by prayer. God's days of power are when God's church comes into its mightiest inheritance of mightiest faith and mightiest prayer. God's conquering days are when God's saints have given themselves to the mightiest prayer.

PROMISES

ON PRAYER

This is the confidence we have in approaching God: that if we ask anything according to his will, he hears us.

1 John 5:14, NIV

To Seth also a son was born, and he called his name Enosh. At that time people began to call upon the name of the LORD.

Genesis 4:26, ESV

Hear me when I call, O God of my righteousness! You have relieved me in my distress; have mercy on me, and hear my prayer. The LORD will hear when I call to Him.

Psalm 4:1, 3, NKJV

If my people, who are called by my name, will humble themselves and pray and seek my face and turn from their wicked ways, then will I hear from heaven and will forgive their sin and will heal their land.

2 Chronicles 7:14, NIV

Hear the voice of my supplications when I cry to You, when I lift up my hands toward Your holy sanctuary.

Psalm 28:2, NKJV

I sought the LORD, and he heard me, and delivered me from all my fears.

Psalm 34:4, KJV

You will call upon Me and go and pray to Me, and I will listen to you. And you will seek Me and find Me, when you search for Me with all your heart.

Jeremiah 29:12-13, NKJV

"I tell you, whatever you ask for in prayer, believe that you have received it, and it will be yours. And when you stand praying, if you hold anything against anyone, forgive him, so that your Father in heaven may forgive you your sins."

Mark 11:24-25, NIV

"Whatever you ask in my name, this I will do, that the Father may be glorified in the Son. If you ask me anything in my name, I will do it."

John 14:13-14, ESV

For this reason I kneel before the Father, from whom his whole family in heaven and on earth derives its name. I pray that out of his glorious riches he may strengthen you with power through his Spirit in your inner being.

Ephesians 3:14-16, NIV

"And I say unto you, Ask, and it shall be given you; seek, and ye shall find; knock, and it shall be opened unto you. For every one that asketh receiveth; and he that seeketh findeth; and to him that knocketh it shall be opened."

Luke 11:9-10, KJV

"And when you pray, you must not be like the hypocrites. For they love to stand and pray in the synagogues and at the street corners, that they may be seen by others. Truly, I say to you, they have received their reward. But when you pray, go into your room and shut the door and pray to your Father who is in secret. And your Father who sees in secret will reward you. your Father knows what you need before you ask him."

Matthew 6:5-6, 8, ESV

REJECTION

Those who know Your name will put their trust in You; for You, LORD, have not forsaken those who seek You.

Psalm 9:10, NKJV

The loneliness of being excluded from a community can be extremely painful. Many people undergo the distressing experience of being passed over for promotion or dismissed from their jobs because of their age. When you find yourself in such a situation, turn to Him who knows and understands only too well what it means to be rejected. He was sent by God to bring the message of God's love to humanity. Yet He was despised and forsaken by people. Despite His physical, mental and emotional suffering, they could not break His spirit.

Whatever you may suffer because of people's changeability, Jesus' love for you remains a constant. Hold on to this immovable truth, and through Jesus Christ you will be able to deal with your feelings of rejection and feel how His love fills your life and your heart.

THE WORD'S RESPONSE

TO REJECTION

When the poor and needy seek water, and there is none, and their tongue faileth for thirst, I the LORD will hear them, I the God of Israel will not forsake them.

Isaiah 41:17, KJV

Be strong and of good courage, do not fear nor be afraid of them; for the LORD your God, He is the One who goes with you. He will not leave you nor forsake you.

Deuteronomy 31:6, NKJV

For the LORD thy God is a merciful God; he will not forsake thee, neither destroy thee, nor forget the covenant of thy fathers which he sware unto them.

Deuteronomy 4:31, KJV

You received the Spirit of sonship. And by him we cry, "Abba, Father." The Spirit himself testifies with our spirit that we are God's children.

Romans 8:15-16, NIV

For the LORD will not cast off his people, neither will he forsake his inheritance.

Psalm 94:14, KJV

He was despised and rejected by men; a man of sorrows, and acquainted with grief; and as one from whom men hide their faces he was despised, and we esteemed him not. Surely he has borne our griefs and carried our sorrows; yet we esteemed him stricken, smitten by God, and afflicted.

Isaiah 53:3-4, ESV

"Can a mother forget the baby at her breast and have no compassion on the child she has borne? Though she may forget, I will not forget you! See, I have engraved you on the palms of my hands; your walls are ever before me."

Isaiah 49:15-16, NIV

Even my close friend in whom I trusted, who ate my bread, has lifted his heel against me. But you, O LORD, be gracious to me, and raise me up, that I may repay them! By this I know that you delight in me: my enemy will not shout in triumph over me.

Psalm 41:9-11, ESV

The LORD will not forsake His people, for His great name's sake, because it has pleased the LORD to make you His people.

1 Samuel 12:22, NKJV

He remembers His covenant forever, the word which He commanded, for a thousand generations, the covenant which He made with Abraham, and His oath to Isaac, and confirmed it to Jacob for a statute, to Israel as an everlasting covenant.

Psalm 105:8-10, NKJV

Know therefore that the LORD your God is God, the faithful God who keeps covenant and steadfast love with those who love him and keep his commandments, to a thousand generations.

Deuteronomy 7:9, ESV

God is not a man, that he should lie; neither the son of man, that he should repent: hath he said, and shall he not do it? or hath he spoken, and shall he not make it good?

Numbers 23:19, KJV

$\mathcal{S}$ALVATION

"Sirs, what must I do to be saved?" So they said, "Believe on the Lord Jesus Christ, and you will be saved, you and your household."
Acts 16:30-31, NKJV

Jesus Christ took the sins of the world upon Himself and bore them in atonement for us. God took our unrighteousness upon Him; our punishment was upon Him; by His wounds we were healed.

What is God's wrath? It is the all-consuming blaze of His holiness that works to destroy sin. Some people do not want to hear anything about God's wrath. God is love, they say. But God is also holy and we dare not consider His holiness as less important than His love. Wrath is at its most severe when it is justly conveyed by love. God is just in His love. Therefore, He could not let sin go unpunished.

Look at Christ in His incomparable sorrow, brought upon Him by a just God in His wrath. Our God, who is endlessly just, is also endlessly great in love and grace. That is our hope and our salvation.

GOD'S PROMISE

OF SALVATION

They shall not defile themselves anymore with their idols, nor with their detestable things, nor with any of their transgressions; but I will deliver them from all their dwelling places in which they have sinned, and will cleanse them. Then they shall be My people, and I will be their God.

Ezekiel 37:23, NKJV

"And there is salvation in no one else, for there is no other name under heaven given among men by which we must be saved."

Acts 4:12, ESV

"And this is the will of Him who sent Me, that everyone who sees the Son and believes in Him may have everlasting life; and I will raise him up at the last day."

John 6:40, NKJV

Lead me in thy truth, and teach me: for thou art the God of my salvation; on thee do I wait all the day.

Psalm 25:5, KJV

Deliver me from all my transgressions: make me not the reproach of the foolish.

Psalm 39:8, KJV

Because of his great love for us, God, who is rich in mercy, made us alive with Christ even when we were dead in transgressions – it is by grace you have been saved. For it is by grace you have been saved, through faith – and this not from yourselves, it is the gift of God – not by works, so that no one can boast.

Ephesians 2:4-5, 8-9, NIV

For the grace of God that bringeth salvation hath appeared to all men. Looking for that blessed hope, and the glorious appearing of the great God and our Saviour Jesus Christ; Who gave himself for us, that he might redeem us from all iniquity, and purify unto himself a peculiar people, zealous of good works.

Titus 2:11, 13-14, KJV

To him give all the prophets witness, that through his name whosoever believeth in him shall receive remission of sins.

Acts 10:43, KJV

If anyone is in Christ, he is a new creation; old things have passed away; behold, all things have become new.

2 Corinthians 5:17, NKJV

For whosoever shall call upon the name of the Lord shall be saved.

Romans 10:13, KJV

"She will give birth to a son, and you are to give him the name Jesus, because he will save his people from their sins."

Matthew 1:21, NIV

"For God so loved the world that He gave His only begotten Son, that whoever believes in Him should not perish but have everlasting life. For God did not send His Son into the world to condemn the world, but that the world through Him might be saved."

John 3:16-17, NKJV

And we have seen and testify that the Father has sent his Son to be the Savior of the world.

1 John 4:14, ESV

$\mathcal{S}$ELF~WORTH

You are the temple of the living God.
2 Corinthians 6:16, NKJV

It is surprising how many people try to be someone else. It is often a subconscious response to the influence of people they consider to be important. Opinions, language, and attitudes tend to conform to that of the company that you keep. Often we are scared to be "different".

It is good to remind yourself that God created you to be a unique, different person. God does not make duplicates. He gave you your very own personality and mind as well as the ability to utilize and develop these. More than that, He has given us each a free will so that we can determine our own actions and conduct.

Don't allow other people to unduly influence you, especially regarding the special gifts that God has given you. Maintain close fellowship with Jesus and allow His Holy Spirit to control your thoughts and actions. Then you will live confidently and earn the respect and esteem of others.

The Word's view

on self-worth

I praise you, for I am fearfully and wonderfully made. Wonderful are your works; my soul knows it very well. My frame was not hidden from you, when I was being made in secret, intricately woven in the depths of the earth. Your eyes saw my unformed substance; in your book were written, every one of them, the days that were formed for me, when as yet there were none of them.

Psalm 139:14-16, ESV

We are heirs – heirs of God and co-heirs with Christ, if indeed we share in his sufferings in order that we may also share in his glory.

Romans 8:17, NIV

Know that the LORD, he is God! It is he who made us, and we are his; we are his people, and the sheep of his pasture.

Psalm 100:3, ESV

Wherefore thou art no more a servant, but a son; and if a son, then an heir of God through Christ.

Galatians 4:7, KJV

"Are not two sparrows sold for a farthing? and one of them shall not fall on the ground without your Father. But the very hairs of your head are all numbered. Fear ye not therefore, ye are of more value than many sparrows."

Matthew 10:29-31, KJV

But you are a chosen race, a royal priesthood, a holy nation, a people for his own possession, that you may proclaim the excellencies of him who called you out of darkness into his marvelous light.

1 Peter 2:9, ESV

What is man, that thou art mindful of him? and the son of man, that thou visitest him? For thou hast made him a little lower than the angels, and hast crowned him with glory and honour. Thou madest him to have dominion over the works of thy hands; thou hast put all things under his feet.

Psalm 8:4-6, KJV

"The Father himself loves you, because you have loved me and have believed that I came from God."

John 16:27, ESV

But the LORD said to Samuel, "Do not look at his appearance or at his physical stature, because I have refused him. For the LORD does not see as man sees; for man looks at the outward appearance, but the LORD looks at the heart."

1 Samuel 16:7, NKJV

See, I have inscribed you on the palms of My hands; your walls are continually before Me.

Isaiah 49:16, NKJV

There is neither Jew nor Greek, there is neither bond nor free, there is neither male nor female: for ye are all one in Christ Jesus.

Galatians 3:28, KJV

So God created man in his own image, in the image of God he created him; male and female he created them.

Genesis 1:27, ESV

He chose us in him before the creation of the world to be holy and blameless in his sight. In love he predestined us to be adopted as his sons through Jesus Christ.

Ephesians 1:4-5, NIV

ᔕHAME

Purge me with hyssop, and I shall be clean; wash me, and I shall be whiter than snow.

Psalm 51:7, ESV

An exaggerated feeling of guilt can become a dangerous and destructive emotion in your life. The greatest danger is that you can become so used to it that you later accept it as a normal emotion. Then your life will become empty and dull and you will lose your enthusiasm for the things of God. If you suffer from a guilt complex you will no longer enjoy life the way God intended.

If you are bowed down under the weight of guilt, you do have reason to thank God. It is proof that you are not insensitive to His presence. A person who does not feel remorse has become deaf to the voice of the Holy Spirit and is no longer sensitive to God's will.

Repent and confess your sins to God, acknowledging that He is able to forgive you and renew your relationship with Him. Then the burden of guilt will be lifted.

THE WORD'S ANSWER

TO SHAME

Unto thee, O LORD, do I lift up my soul. O my God, I trust in thee: let me not be ashamed, let not mine enemies triumph over me. Yea, let none that wait on thee be ashamed: let them be ashamed which transgress without cause.

Psalm 25:1-3, KJV

But Israel is saved by the LORD with everlasting salvation; you shall not be put to shame or confounded to all eternity.

Isaiah 45:17, ESV

I sought the LORD, and he heard me, and delivered me from all my fears. They looked unto him, and were lightened: and their faces were not ashamed.

Psalm 34:4-5, KJV

With the heart one believes unto righteousness, and with the mouth confession is made unto salvation. For the Scripture says, "Whoever believes on Him will not be put to shame."

Romans 10:10-11, NKJV

May my heart be blameless in your statutes, that I may not be put to shame!

Psalm 119:80, ESV

In Scripture it says: "See, I lay a stone in Zion, a chosen and precious cornerstone, and the one who trusts in him will never be put to shame."

1 Peter 2:6, NIV

Fear not; for thou shalt not be ashamed: neither be thou confounded; for thou shalt not be put to shame: for thou shalt forget the shame of thy youth, and shalt not remember the reproach of thy widowhood any more.

Isaiah 54:4, KJV

Consecrate yourselves therefore, and be holy, for I am the LORD your God. And you shall keep My statutes, and perform them: I am the LORD who sanctifies you.

Leviticus 20:7-8, NKJV

Draw nigh unto my soul, and redeem it: deliver me because of mine enemies. Thou hast known my reproach, and my shame, and my dishonour: mine adversaries are all before thee.

Psalm 69:18-19, KJV

"You are already clean because of the word which I have spoken to you."

John 15:3-4, NKJV

Christ loved the church and gave himself up for her to make her holy, cleansing her by the washing with water through the word, and to present her to himself as a radiant church, without stain or wrinkle or any other blemish, but holy and blameless.

Ephesians 5:25-27, NIV

To her it was granted to be arrayed in fine linen, clean and bright, for the fine linen is the righteous acts of the saints.

Revelation 19:8, NKJV

"For whoever is ashamed of me and of my words, of him will the Son of Man be ashamed when he comes in his glory and the glory of the Father and of the holy angels."

Luke 9:26, ESV

And I will cleanse them from all their iniquity, whereby they have sinned against me; and I will pardon all their iniquities, whereby they have sinned, and whereby they have transgressed against me.

Jeremiah 33:8, KJV

$\mathscr{S}$IN

Wretched man that I am! Who will deliver me from this body of death? Thanks be to God through Jesus Christ our Lord!

Romans 7:24-25, ESV

On your way to spiritual maturity, you cannot avoid the awfulness of sin. This is the saddest fact about human life. But the most glorious fact about God is that, although He hates sin, He loves the sinner. He is a God of abundant love and grace.

The Heidelberg Catechism states that a prerequisite for a happy life and a peaceful death is that we need to know the extent of our sin and how utterly lost we really are.

These days it is not fashionable to talk about sin. Sin is excused in a multitude of terms: nervous tension; psychological disturbance; an aberration; mental illness, or human weakness. However, if we replace the label on a jar of poison with the word "Honey" it remains deadly poisonous.

There is but one solution for sin: Christ. *"He will forgive us our sins and purify us from all unrighteousness"* (John 1:9, NIV).

The Word's view

on sin

For all have sinned and fall short of the glory of God, and are justified by his grace as a gift, through the redemption that is in Christ Jesus, whom God put forward as a propitiation by his blood, to be received by faith. This was to show God's righteousness, because in his divine forbearance he had passed over former sins.

Romans 3:23-25, ESV

Therefore if any man be in Christ, he is a new creature: old things are passed away; behold, all things are become new. And all things are of God, who hath reconciled us to himself by Jesus Christ, and hath given to us the ministry of reconciliation; To wit, that God was in Christ, reconciling the world unto himself, not imputing their trespasses unto them.

2 Corinthians 5:17-19, KJV

If we confess our sins, he is faithful and just to forgive us our sins, and to cleanse us from all unrighteousness.

1 John 1:9, NIV

Let love be genuine. Abhor what is evil; hold fast to what is good.

Romans 12:9, ESV

Just as man is destined to die once, and after that to face judgment, so Christ was sacrificed once to take away the sins of many people; and he will appear a second time, not to bear sin, but to bring salvation to those who are waiting for him.

Hebrews 9:27-28, NIV

He himself bore our sins in his body on the tree, that we might die to sin and live to righteousness. By his wounds you have been healed.

1 Peter 2:24, ESV

I know that nothing good lives in me, that is, in my sinful nature. For I have the desire to do what is good, but I cannot carry it out. For what I do is not the good I want to do; no, the evil I do not want to do – this I keep on doing. Now if I do what I do not want to do, it is no longer I who do it, but it is sin living in me that does it. So I find this law at work: When I want to do good, evil is right there with me.

Romans 7:18-21, NIV

Therefore if any man be in Christ, he is a new creature: old things are passed away; behold, all things are become new.

2 Corinthians 5:17, KJV

What shall we say then? Are we to continue in sin that grace may abound? By no means! How can we who died to sin still live in it? Do you not know that all of us who have been baptized into Christ Jesus were baptized into his death? We know that our old self was crucified with him in order that the body of sin might be brought to nothing, so that we would no longer be enslaved to sin.

Romans 6:1-3, 6, ESV

Who shall bring a charge against God's elect? It is God who justifies. Who is he who condemns? It is Christ who died, and furthermore is also risen, who is even at the right hand of God, who also makes intercession for us.

Romans 8:33-34, NKJV

I acknowledged my sin to you, and I did not cover my iniquity; I said, "I will confess my transgressions to the LORD," and you forgave the iniquity of my sin.

Psalm 32:5, ESV

$\mathscr{S}$TRESS

Do not be anxious about tomorrow, for tomorrow will be anxious for itself.
        Matthew 6:34, ESV

Life makes increasingly heavy demands on us. As situations threaten to overwhelm you, tension builds up in your heart and mind, resulting in insomnia, touchiness and depression.

Preventing tension is easier than dealing with its symptoms. To prevent tension from becoming unbearable, you need to develop a meaningful life of prayer. Time quietly spent with God lifts the lid off the pressure cooker and releases calmness and balance. His Holy Presence then permeates your life in blessing and enrichment. The tension dissipates in His presence.

The Lord leads you to an oasis of peace and tranquility. There is rest and renewal in times of prayer. From the eddying whirlpool of life that threatens to rob you of your peace of mind, God brings you to the quiet of His holy fellowship. There you will find deliverance and healing.

THE WORD'S ANSWER

TO STRESS

We are afflicted in every way, but not crushed; perplexed, but not driven to despair; persecuted, but not forsaken; struck down, but not destroyed; always carrying in the body the death of Jesus, so that the life of Jesus may also be manifested in our bodies. So we do not lose heart. Though our outer nature is wasting away, our inner nature is being renewed day by day. For this slight momentary affliction is preparing for us an eternal weight of glory beyond all comparison, as we look not to the things that are seen but to the things that are unseen. For the things that are seen are transient, but the things that are unseen are eternal.

2 Corinthians 4:8-10, 16-18, ESV

Though I walk in the midst of trouble, You will revive me; You will stretch out Your hand against the wrath of my enemies, and Your right hand will save me.

Psalm 138:7, NKJV

We glory in tribulations also: knowing that tribulation worketh patience; and patience, experience; and experience, hope.

Romans 5:3-4, KJV

My brethren, count it all joy when you fall into various trials, knowing that the testing of your faith produces patience. But let patience have its perfect work, that you may be perfect and complete, lacking nothing.

James 1:2-4, NKJV

Blessed is the man who perseveres under trial, because when he has stood the test, he will receive the crown of life that God has promised to those who love him.

James 1:12, NIV

Fear not, for I am with you; be not dismayed, for I am your God; I will strengthen you, I will help you, I will uphold you with my righteous right hand.

Isaiah 41:10, ESV

Humble yourselves therefore under the mighty hand of God, that he may exalt you in due time: Casting all your care upon him; for he careth for you.

1 Peter 5:6-7, KJV

Be anxious for nothing, but in everything by prayer and supplication, with thanksgiving, let your requests be made known to God; and the peace of God, which surpasses all understanding, will guard your hearts and minds through Christ Jesus.

Philippians 4:6-7, NKJV

I can do all things through him who strengthens me.

Philippians 4:13, ESV

"Come to me, all who labor and are heavy laden, and I will give you rest. Take my yoke upon you, and learn from me, for I am gentle and lowly in heart, and you will find rest for your souls. For my yoke is easy, and my burden is light."

Matthew 11:28-30, ESV

He gives power to the faint, and to him who has no might he increases strength. Even youths shall faint and be weary, and young men shall fall exhausted; but they who wait for the LORD shall renew their strength; they shall mount up with wings like eagles; they shall run and not be weary; they shall walk and not faint.

Isaiah 40:29-31, ESV

TEMPTATION

Because he himself suffered when he was tempted,
he is able to help those who are being tempted.

Hebrews 2:18, NIV

If they are totally honest, most Christians will acknowledge that they experience problems living in obedience to the commands of the Master. Some go through barren patches of the spirit and struggle with the temptation to compromise with the sinful world.

Jesus was exposed to immense temptations. There were moments, like shortly before His crucifixion, when a compromise of His principles would have been greatly advantageous to His human welfare. If He had given in, He would have been spared the horror of the cross, but He would have robbed Himself of the glory of the resurrection, and the world of salvation. Just as Jesus drew His strength from the Spirit of God, He proffers His Holy Spirit to you to enable you to triumph over temptation and to live as He wants you to live. Open your life to the Holy Spirit and remain sensitive and obedient to Him at all times.

THE WORD'S VIEW

ON TEMPTATION

My brethren, count it all joy when you fall into various trials, knowing that the testing of your faith produces patience.

James 1:2-3, NKJV

No temptation has seized you except what is common to man. And God is faithful; he will not let you be tempted beyond what you can bear. But when you are tempted, he will also provide a way out so that you can stand up under it.

1 Corinthians 10:13, NIV

The Lord knoweth how to deliver the godly out of temptations, and to reserve the unjust unto the day of judgment to be punished.

2 Peter 2:9, KJV

"Watch and pray, lest you enter into temptation. The spirit indeed is willing, but the flesh is weak."

Mark 14:38, NKJV

You, dear children, are from God and have overcome them, because the one who is in you is greater than the one who is in the world.

1 John 4:4, NIV

Flee the evil desires of youth, and pursue righteousness, faith, love and peace, along with those who call on the Lord out of a pure heart.

2 Timothy 2:22, NIV

Be strong in the Lord and in the power of His might. Put on the whole armor of God, that you may be able to stand against the wiles of the devil. For we do not wrestle against flesh and blood, but against principalities, against powers, against the rulers of the darkness of this age, against spiritual hosts of wickedness in the heavenly places. Therefore take up the whole armor of God, that you may be able to withstand in the evil day, and having done all, to stand.

Ephesians 6:10-13, NKJV

Be sober, be vigilant; because your adversary the devil, as a roaring lion, walketh about, seeking whom he may devour.

1 Peter 5:8, KJV

Submit yourselves therefore to God. Resist the devil, and he will flee from you. Draw nigh to God, and he will draw nigh to you.

James 4:7-8, KJV

We do not have a high priest who is unable to sympathize with our weaknesses, but we have one who has been tempted in every way, just as we are – yet was without sin. Let us then approach the throne of grace with confidence, so that we may receive mercy and find grace to help us in our time of need.

Hebrews 4:15-16, NIV

Let no one say when he is tempted, "I am being tempted by God," for God cannot be tempted with evil, and he himself tempts no one. But each person is tempted when he is lured and enticed by his own desire.

James 1:13-14, ESV

"Woe to the world for temptations to sin! For it is necessary that temptations come, but woe to the one by whom the temptation comes!"

Matthew 18:7, ESV

$\mathcal{T}$RUST

I will wait for the LORD, who is hiding his face from the house of Jacob. I will put my trust in him.

Isaiah 8:17, NIV

The Bible is full of the ways that God was faithful to His promises. Therefore, we can trust Him in every area of life. But you cannot force God's hand or hurry Him along. He works according to His perfect time and methods. Even though your life might seem chaotic to you, remember that He has an overall picture of your life. He is all-seeing and all-knowing. Your faith in His goodness should give you an unshakeable trust in His promises, and so you will be able to wait for His decisions.

When dark days come, keep trusting Him. Seek the guidance of the Holy Spirit. Ask Him for the power to discern so that you can see the answers to your prayers. You can, with childlike trust, leave everything in His hands. You can trust Him to provide for you. They who stand steadfast in affliction, receive God's most precious gifts from His treasure house of mercy.

TRUST IN GOD

Trust in the LORD with all thine heart; and lean not unto thine own understanding. In all thy ways acknowledge him, and he shall direct thy paths.

Proverbs 3:5-6, KJV

O my God, in you I trust; let me not be put to shame; let not my enemies exult over me.

Psalm 25:2, ESV

"I tell you the truth, anyone who has faith in me will do what I have been doing. He will do even greater things than these, because I am going to the Father. And I will do whatever you ask in my name, so that the Son may bring glory to the Father. You may ask me for anything in my name, and I will do it."

John 14:12-14, NIV

It is better to trust in the LORD than to put confidence in man. It is better to trust in the LORD than to put confidence in princes.

Psalm 118:8-9, NKJV

Trust ye in the LORD for ever: for in the LORD Jehovah is everlasting strength.

Isaiah 26:4, KJV

Some trust in chariots, and some in horses; but we will remember the name of the LORD our God.

Psalm 20:7, NKJV

Now faith is being sure of what we hope for and certain of what we do not see. This is what the ancients were commended for. By faith we understand that the universe was formed at God's command, so that what is seen was not made out of what was visible.

Hebrews 11:1-3, NIV

When I am afraid, I put my trust in you. In God, whose word I praise, in God I trust; I shall not be afraid. What can flesh do to me?

Psalm 56:3-4, ESV

The LORD is good, a stronghold in the day of trouble; and He knows those who trust in Him.

Nahum 1:7, NKJV

"Assuredly, I say to you, if you have faith and do not doubt, you will not only do what was done to the fig tree, but also if you say to this mountain, 'Be removed and be cast into the sea,' it will be done. And whatever things you ask in prayer, believing, you will receive."

Matthew 21:21-22, NKJV

"Surely God is my salvation; I will trust and not be afraid. The LORD, the LORD, is my strength and my song; he has become my salvation."

Isaiah 12:2, NIV

Who is among you that feareth the LORD, that obeyeth the voice of his servant, that walketh in darkness, and hath no light? let him trust in the name of the LORD, and stay upon his God.

Isaiah 50:10, KJV

The God of my rock; in him will I trust: he is my shield, and the horn of my salvation, my high tower, and my refuge, my saviour; thou savest me from violence.

2 Samuel 22:3, KJV

WHY ME?

The LORD will fulfill his purpose for me; your love, O LORD, endures forever – do not abandon the works of your hands.

Psalm 138:8, NIV

Do you live in a world of shattered dreams where everything has collapsed like a house of cards? You once had a dream that inspired you but now everything has gone wrong.

You can lapse into self-pity and bemoan your sad fate to all who will listen. You can convince yourself that you are a loser and that you will never succeed again.

But perhaps you should ask yourself some heart-searching questions. Why did you experience failure? Did you over-estimate your abilities? Have the courage to face the truth about yourself and your situation and do something positive about it. The world is full of people who succeeded only after many attempts. God sometimes allows failure to put us on a different path. Trust Him with His plan for your life. Persevere and you will burst through the barriers of failure to experience true success.

GOD'S ANSWER
TO "WHY ME?"

In this you greatly rejoice, though now for a little while you may have had to suffer grief in all kinds of trials. These have come so that your faith – of greater worth than gold, which perishes even though refined by fire – may be proved genuine and may result in praise, glory and honor when Jesus Christ is revealed.

1 Peter 1:6-7, NIV

Beloved, think it not strange concerning the fiery trial which is to try you, as though some strange thing happened unto you: But rejoice, inasmuch as ye are partakers of Christ's sufferings; that, when his glory shall be revealed, ye may be glad also with exceeding joy.

1 Peter 4:12-13, KJV

Behold, I have refined you, but not as silver; I have tried you in the furnace of affliction.

Isaiah 48:10, ESV

Not only so, but we also rejoice in our sufferings, because we know that suffering produces perseverance; perseverance, character; and character, hope. And hope does not disappoint us, because God has poured out his love into our hearts by the Holy Spirit, whom he has given us.

Romans 5:3-5, NIV

Blessed be the God and Father of our Lord Jesus Christ, the Father of mercies and God of all comfort, who comforts us in all our tribulation, that we may be able to comfort those who are in any trouble, with the comfort with which we ourselves are comforted by God. For as the sufferings of Christ abound in us, so our consolation also abounds through Christ.

2 Corinthians 1:3-5, NKJV

Consider it pure joy, my brothers, whenever you face trials of many kinds, because you know that the testing of your faith develops perseverance. Perseverance must finish its work so that you may be mature and complete, not lacking anything.

James 1:2-4, NIV

Recall the former days in which, after you were illuminated, you endured a great struggle with sufferings: partly while you were made a spectacle both by reproaches and tribulations, and partly while you became companions of those who were so treated; for you had compassion on me in my chains, and joyfully accepted the plundering of your goods, knowing that you have a better and an enduring possession for yourselves in heaven. Therefore do not cast away your confidence, which has great reward.

Hebrews 10:32-35, NKJV

"Do not remember the former things, nor consider the things of old. Behold, I will do a new thing, now it shall spring forth; shall you not know it? I will even make a road in the wilderness and rivers in the desert."

Isaiah 43:18-19, NKJV

Beloved, now are we the sons of God, and it doth not yet appear what we shall be: but we know that, when he shall appear, we shall be like him; for we shall see him as he is.

1 John 3:2, KJV

WORRY

Call upon Me in the day of trouble; I will deliver you, and you shall glorify Me.

Psalm 50:15, NKJV

Doubt, fear and worry are notorious for the havoc they can wreak on a person's spiritual and emotional well-being. Even stable and clear-headed people can be reduced to confused wrecks through acute anxiety.

How often have you, or someone you know, been confronted with an unmanageable situation? There are no obvious solutions and so a feeling of helplessness and despair develops. In order to handle situa-tions like these and to prevent stumbling over the obstacles of poor advice, you have to trust Christ unconditionally. Lay yourself and your concerns before Him and allow Him to guide you in His way.

With God everything is possible, and as you come to live more intimately with Christ, you will find that He will guide you safely through each crisis. He will give you His peace, the peace that is beyond all human comprehension.

THE WORD'S

RESPONSE TO WORRY

Humble yourselves, therefore, under God's mighty hand, that he may lift you up in due time. Cast all your anxiety on him because he cares for you. Be self-controlled and alert. Your enemy the devil prowls around like a roaring lion looking for someone to devour. Resist him, standing firm in the faith, because you know that your brothers throughout the world are undergoing the same kind of sufferings. And the God of all grace, who called you to his eternal glory in Christ, after you have suffered a little while, will himself restore you and make you strong, firm and steadfast. To him be the power for ever and ever.

1 Peter 5:6-11, NIV

Why are you cast down, O my soul, and why are you in turmoil within me? Hope in God; for I shall again praise him, my salvation and my God.

Psalm 42:11, ESV

Now may our Lord Jesus Christ Himself, and our God and Father, who has loved us and given us everlasting consolation and good hope by grace, comfort your hearts and establish you in every good word and work.

2 Thessalonians 2:16-17, NKJV

Ah Lord God! behold, thou hast made the heaven and the earth by thy great power and stretched out arm, and there is nothing too hard for thee.

Jeremiah 32:17, KJV

Our help is in the name of the LORD, who made heaven and earth.

Psalm 124:8, NKJV

If God is for us, who can be against us? He who did not spare His own Son, but delivered Him up for us all, how shall He not with Him also freely give us all things?

Romans 8:31-32, NKJV

If I say, "My foot slips," your mercy, O Lord, will hold me up. In the multitude of my anxieties within me, your comforts delight my soul.

Psalm 94:18-19, NKJV

In my distress I called upon the LORD, and cried unto my God: he heard my voice out of his temple, and my cry came before him, even into his ears. He sent from above, he took me, he drew me out of many waters. He delivered me from my strong enemy, and from them which hated me: for they were too strong for me.

Psalm 18: 6, 16-17, KJV

Be anxious for nothing, but in everything by prayer and supplication, with thanksgiving, let your requests be made known to God; and the peace of God, which surpasses all understanding, will guard your hearts and minds through Christ Jesus.

Philippians 4:6-7, NKJV

"Therefore do not be anxious, saying, 'What shall we eat?' or 'What shall we drink?' or 'What shall we wear?' For the Gentiles seek after all these things, and your heavenly Father knows that you need them all."

Matthew 6:31-32, ESV

Cast your burden on the LORD, and He shall sustain you; He shall never permit the righteous to be moved.

Psalm 55:22, NKJV

Sources

The devotions included in this book have been drawn from the following sources:

1. Harvey, E and L. eds. 2002. *Kneeling we Triumph.* Vereeniging: Christian Art Publishers.
2. Mitchell, Fred. 1968. *At Break of Day.* Marshall: Morgan and Scott.
3. Ozrovech, Solly. 2002. *Fountains of Blessing.* Vereeniging: Christian Art Publishers.
4. Ozrovech, Solly. 1995. *The Glory of God's Grace.* Vereeniging: Christian Art Publishers.
5. Ozrovech, Solly. 2000. *Intimate Moments with God.* Vereeniging: Christian Art Publishers.
6. Ozrovech, Solly. 2002. *New Beginnings.* Vereeniging: Christian Art Publishers.
7. Ozrovech, Solly. 2002. *The Voice Behind You.* Vereeniging: Christian Art Publishers.
8. Shaw, Nola. 2003. *Does God Love the Divorcée?* Vereeniging: Christian Art Publishers.
9. Shaw, Nola. 2002. *The Valley of Tears.* Vereeniging: Christian Art Publishers.

OTHER BOOKS
IN THIS RANGE

ISBN: 1-86920-072-1

ISBN: 1-86920-069-1

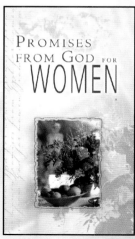

ISBN: 1-86920-070-5